Silver

Silver

A PRACTICAL GUIDE TO
COLLECTING SILVERWARE AND
IDENTIFYING HALLMARKS

JOEL LANGFORD

SELECT
EDITIONS

A QUANTUM BOOK

Paperback edition published by
Selectabook Ltd.
Selectabook Distribution Centre,
Folly Road,
Roundway,
Devizes
Wiltshire SN10 2HR

This edition printed 2004

ISBN 1-86160-972-8

QUMCSM

This book is produced by
Quantum Publishing Ltd.
6 Blundell Street
London N7 9BH

Printed in Singapore
by Star Standard Industries Pte Ltd

ACKNOWLEDGMENT
A very special thank you is owed to Dorothy T. Rainwater, author of the invaluable "Encyclopedia of American Silver Manufacturers". Without her diligent research this book would not have been possible.

Contents

Glossary of terms

We are beginning this book with a glossary since, with the passage of time, many of the terms used to describe the process of manufacturing, decorating and making silver have become corrupted or misused. This has caused much confusion for those trying to understand the subject. This basic glossary endeavours to provide simple definitions of the terms used in the silver business. A special section at the end helps to identify silver objects which are unusual or no longer in common use.

GENERAL TERMS

APPLIED DECORATION A term for any decoration (such as swags and garlands), stampings or castings made independently from the main body of the piece and then attached to it.

ASSAY The compulsory process of testing the purity of metals. Taken from the Old French word *assai,* meaning examination or trial. All silversmiths are required to register their marks and details with an assay office and submit all work for examination. If the pure silver content is as represented, the work is officially stamped or hallmarked, by the local assay office. If not, the item is confiscated and in most cases destroyed.

BALUSTER A decorative pillar or stem. Examples are found on candlesticks, wine cups and goblets.

'BLACKSMITH'S REPAIRS' Rudimentary solder-and-patch repairs, often carried out by the village blacksmith or by craftworker other than a skilled silversmith.

BRIGHT-CUT ENGRAVING A facet-cut decoration, particularly popular in the 18th and early-19th centuries.

BRITANNIA METAL Made from copper, tin and regulus of antimony, this alloy is of similar appearance to silver or polished pewter. Used from *c.* 1840.

BRITANNIA STANDARD One of the only two standards of silver allowed in Britain (see sterling silver below). This higher standard (958 parts silver) for wrought silver was introduced by law in 1697 and remained in use until 1720. It replaced the sterling standard during this period and was introduced to prevent the melting or partial clipping of coinage to satisfy the post-Civil War demand for silver plate. Most plate had been melted and turned into coins during the Civil War. The Restoration period saw a greater demand for plate than even before the war, which subsequently created a shortage of coins.

BURNISHING A lustrous effect created on silver or other metals by the use of a hard, smooth tool made of agate. However from the early 1800s, machine-polishing slowly began to be the most popular technique for achieving a shine. Today burnishing is only occasionally undertaken.

CARTOUCHE Tablet ornament, usually oval in shape, with a decorative or scrolled edge. The centre depicts a coat of arms, a design or an inscription.

CHASING The highly skilled art of hammering metal in order to produce either a relief or an indented pattern without incurring any metal loss.

CHASED UP A chiselling technique used to finish cast objects.

CLOSE-PLATE Used during the 18th century for everyday objects such as spurs, knife blades and buckles. A thin foil of silver was soldered onto polished steel which had been dipped into tin. The piece was always burnished. More cost-effective methods rendered this process obsolete during the 19th century.

CUT-CARD DECORATION Pierced applied silverwork decoration usually featuring foliage and often soldered round the body of the object or used as a border. It is frequently paired with beadwork stem decoration.

ELECTRO-FORMING A spin-off of electroplating, where metal is electro-deposited into a mould and removed when sufficient thickness has been achieved to produce a solid, freestanding object. In the silver trade silver, copper or fine gold are used. Copper items are then electroplated. This production method allowed intricate items to be reproduced for a fraction of the cost of their handmade equivalents.

ELECTROPLATING A method of coating an object with silver by passing an electric current through the object and a solution of cyanide of potassium, which causes the silver ions to adhere to the object.

ENGRAVING This well-known decorative technique is achieved by cutting away the silver or metal. Engraving is extremely versatile, lending itself to simple inscriptions or to grandiose decorations.

EPNS Electroplated nickel silver, nickel being the base metal plated.

EPBM Electroplated Britannia metal, Britannia metal being the base metal plated.

FILLED Articles with a central cavity were, and still are, often filled with plaster or other substances to give stability.

LEFT
Cartouche chased on a silver coffee pot, 1860.

FINIAL An adornment found, for instance, on top of a teapot lid or on the tail of a spoon.

FIRE GILDING (MERCURY GILDING) A process in which an amalgam of gold and mercury is painted onto silver. When heated, the mercury volatizes leaving a hard-wearing layer of gold fused to the silver.

FLATWARE The generic term for silver cutlery.

GILDING The application of a thin layer of gold to a metal surface.

GOLD-PLATING The electroplating process is used to apply a thin layer of gold to a metal surface.

HALLMARK A system of marks impressed on silver or gold items by the assay office, the purpose of which is to establish its purity. In Britain, the hallmark consists of the assay mark (lion passant) and other symbols denoting the place of assay, date, and sometimes the makers. The system, with its comprehensive records, also helps the public to identify items and to guard against forgeries. For a more detailed explanation of hallmarks see Chapter 2.

HAND-FORGING The technique of hammering hot metal over an anvil; mostly used for shaping knife blades and other flatware (*q.v.*).

HOLLOW WARE Generic term for items of household silver other than flatware (*q.v.*).

IMPORTED PLATE Foreign silver imported into England was originally assayed and hallmarked on arrival in spite of bearing the marks of its country of origin. In 1844, the law changed to allow foreign silverware made before 1800 be imported without having hallmarks added. Post-1800 pieces still had to be assayed at the port of entry. No identifying mark for this later plate was introduced until 1876.

LACQUERING A coat of lacquer is often given to intricate articles or ceremonial pieces only in occasional use where cleaning is difficult. Fragile objects are sometimes treated in the same way.

LET-IN SHIELD (SILVER SHIELD) As it was not practicable to engrave Old Sheffield Plate because the copper underneath would be exposed, a hole was cut in the object and a solid silver piece or 'shield' of metal was soldered into position.

NIELLO A black alloy used to fill engraved decoration in order to contrast with and enhance the silver. The alloy, consisting of lead, sulphur, copper and silver, is heated and then reduced to granules which can be placed in the cuts of the design and melted until the granules fuse. Any excess is polished away.

OLD SHEFFIELD PLATE Hollow ware (*q. v.*) articles made for domestic use, mainly from copper, and coated with silver by fusion. This fusion method was the accidental invention of a Sheffield cutler in 1743 and enjoyed a production period of 100 years before being superseded by electroplate.

PATINA The beautiful deep, blue-silver lustre silver acquires with the passage of time and numerous surface scratches. This effect is lost by machine-polishing.

PLATE A term used pre-1743 to describe all articles of solid silver and gold. Derived from the Spanish word for silver – *plata* – the term correctly describes all early solid silver, but is often mistakenly used to refer to fused or electroplate.

'PSEUDO' HALLMARKS In 1772 silversmiths protested to stop makers of fused plate using marks resembling those used for sterling silver and configured in the same manner. But, by 1784, fused plate manufacturers were legally allowed to use a maker's name or symbol, commonly known as the maker's mark. However, many carried on using and still use 'pseudo' hallmarks to lend fused plate some of the cachet of silver.

ABOVE
Niello work on Russian casket, 1900.

LEFT
Old Sheffield Plate dish ring *c.* 1790.

QUADRUPLE PLATE An American trade term to suggest the number of times an object is dipped in the plating vat during the electroplating process.

REGISTRATION MARK Introduced around the 1850s in Britain to record the exact date of manufacture of electroplate.

ROLLED EDGE Rolled finish to the edges of Old Sheffield or fused plate articles to conceal the copper middle which would otherwise be visible. The silver was simply folded into a rim or a narrow mount fashioned and soldered to the edge.

SILVER GILT A thin covering of gold over solid silver.

SILVER INLAY A process normally associated with tortoiseshell, whereby the shell is softened by heating and silver patterns pressed into it.

SPINNING A method of producing hollow ware (*q. v.*) by which a flat sheet of silver is fashioned over a shaped wooden chuck fixed to a rotating lathe.

STAND Complementary stands were made for items – including teapots and coffee pots – to protect surfaces such as tabletops from the effects of heat and water.

STERLING SILVER Consists of 925 parts of pure silver to 75 parts of copper. See Britannia standard above.

TINE The prong of a fork.

TINNING A cost-cutting method used in the Old Sheffield

RIGHT

Tankard by William Jones, Marblehead, Massachusetts, 1720–1730, with bead finial

LEFT

Silver tea caddy spoon with gilded shell bowl and open work handle. Caddy spoons usually approximately 2″ in length. Made in 1858.

process where tin is used instead of silver for the interior of, say, a teapot, or the underside of a tray.

TRIPLE PLATE See quadruple plate above. As the name implies, triple plate is one thickness less than quadruple plate and as common.

VERMEIL The French term for silver gilt.

WHALEBONE HANDLE Twisted whalebone was introduced for punch ladles from *c.* 1740 onwards, and used instead of silver and wood.

WHITE METAL A hard alloy of copper and zinc used as an electroplating base.

UNUSUAL OBJECTS

ARGYLL (ARGYLE) Usually used to mean a gravy or sauce boat, or occasionally a meat platter, able to retain the heat of its contents by means of a double-layered sealed jacket or casing. The design is attributed to one of the Dukes of Argyll, possibly the third, hence the name.

BLEEDING BOWL In England, this is a simple shallow dish with a single pierced handle used for letting blood, while in America this type of dish is known as a porringer and was used as a feeding bowl – a much more pleasant function! The English version of porringer always has two handles.

BELOW

Silver-plated chafing dish by Martin Hall & Co, *c.* 1870.

CADDY SPOON For use with a tea caddy, usually approximately 2 inches in length. (*see also* tea caddy)

CHAFING DISH A silver or silver-plated serving bowl with handle and cover. The handles are usually detachable. Many chafing dishes have hot-water jackets (i.e. are double-skinned) and were used to serve either hors d'œuvres or vegetables.

CHÂTELAINE A clip used by the mistress of the house or housekeeper from which hung chains for attaching keys, scissors, needles and other household notions. The châtelaine was hooked on to the wearer's belt and was an object of common use from the Middle Ages until well into the 20th century,

RIGHT

A silver argyle. The contents are kept warm by a double casing filled with hot water.

LEFT

Silver dish cross, 1770, used for keeping dishes hot at the table. Dish crosses were replaced by hot water stands in the 19th century.

although having started as a functional status symbol it became more of a decoration.

DISH OR TABLE CROSS A cross-shaped device with burners for keeping dishes hot while on the table. Adjustable sliding legs and arms meant that dishes of any size could be accommodated. In use from the 1730s to the end of the century, they were replaced by hot-water stands. American examples of dish crosses are extremely rare.

DISH RING A stand with chased or pierced sides to support and elevate dishes. Dishes could only be supported by the size of ring specifically made for them. Dish rings were never very common objects.

EGG BOILER/CODDLER A piece popular during the Victorian era and available primarily in silver plate, used to cook eggs at the table. Boiling water was poured in, the eggs were also placed inside the container within a detachable frame, the cover replaced, and the burner set alight. Approximately seven minutes later, the eggs were ready.

EGG CRUET A frame usually supporting six egg cups and accompanying spoons which often incorporated a container for salt.

ÉPERGNE An ornamental structure, designed to house a central bowl, with branches holding small subsidiary dishes. Candle holders and brackets for containing casters are often additional features. Epergnes were frequently used as table centrepieces, although the name is not a generic term.

LEFT

Silver egg cruet, 1815.

KNIFE REST Traditionally used for carving knives when not in use.

MARROW SCOOP A culinary implement for extracting the marrow from bones.

PAP-BOAT A lipped, boat-shaped child's feeding bowl, first in evidence around 1710 and the 100 years following. It is thought that many have been altered into cream boats.

PORRINGER See bleeding bowl.

QUAICH A shallow, two-handled drinking bowl, originally produced in Scotland. Traditionally, quaiches were made entirely of wood or wood with bands of silver. The word quaich is attributed to the Gaelic word *cuach*, meaning cup.

RÉPOUSSÉ Embossed decorations hammered from behind (as opposed to chasing, hammered from the front).

SPOON WARMER A Victorian invention used at a time when kitchens were often a long way from the dining-room. A variety of articles which could contribute to keeping food warm was

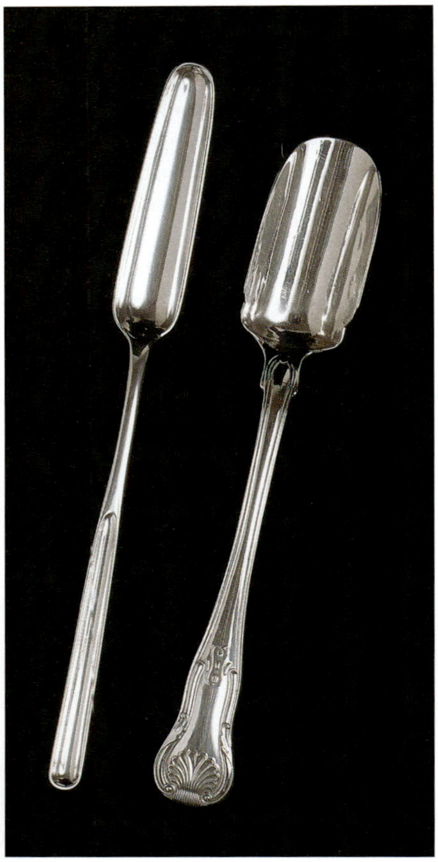

LEFT

Silver marrow scoops made by William Eley and William Fearn, 1799.

OPPOSITE

Silver tea caddy, 1864. By this time tea was less expensive than it had been in the previous century, and there was no longer a need for a lockable lid.

ABOVE

Silver plate and ivory knife rests, *c.* 1880. Traditionally used for carving knives when not in use.

RIGHT

Silver pap boat made by William Bateman, 1819.

RIGHT

Silver quaich, 1923.

BELOW

A pair of matching silver stirrup cups, 1805.

essential. Spoon warmers were generally made in the form of nautalus shells and have small hinged openings. Spoon warmer bases were usually cast to resemble a rock-strewn seabed. The warmer was filled with boiling water and left on the table. All serving spoons were placed in it until needed, enabling them to remain warm in rooms that were so much colder than today.

STIRRUP CUP This was handed to the huntsman before setting off on the hunt.

TANTALUS A descriptive name for a common Victorian piece of sideboard furniture. Its name was derived from a Greek mythological figure, who was subjected to a particularly ingenious form of punishment in Hades which denied him the possibility of quenching his thirst. The 19th-century invention confined individual decanters within a wood or metal frame, with a locking device around the neck and stopper or built into the frame or case. It prevented the household tippling while the master was away. Their popularity continued during the Edwardian period. Some frames in sterling silver can be found, but the majority are either wood – with silver-plated mounts – or silver-plated brass. The glass or crystal decanters vary greatly in quality from cheap pressed glass to the finest, intricately cut crystal.

TAPER STICK These were common implements found on 18th-and 19th-century desks, used to melt wax for sealing letters. They were smaller in height than a candlestick and held a thinner taper than a candle.

TEA CADDY When first imported in the late 1600s, tea was very expensive; this was compounded in the 18th century with heavy taxation, so lockable tea caddies were always in demand. Often the lid was designed for use as a tea scoop or measure.

WALL SCONCE A wall-mounted candlestick.

WAX JACK These were usually silver but were also made in Old Sheffield Plate. Becoming popular in the 18th century, they were kept on the desk and used to melt the sealing wax onto letters and also as an additional form of light. The wax jack frame was fitted with a spiral candle roll made of soft wax which could be extended by twisting the jack handle.

WICK TRIMMER *see photo below.*

ABOVE AND LEFT

Old Sheffield candle wick trimmer and snuffer made by Gilbert & Co *c.* 1830. The scissor action extinguishes the wick and the sprung blade trims it. Not all scissor-type candle snuffers incorporate the wick trimmer.

Silver Standards and Hallmarking

SILVER STANDARDS

The exact origin of the term sterling silver is somewhat hazy. Some believe that it came about because Henry II introduced German silversmiths to England to teach the indigenous smiths their technique for making silver durable. These men were known as Easterlings, having come from the East, and sterling is thought to be a corruption of the word Easterling. Others believe that the term derives from *steorra*, Old English for star; some Norman coins were marked with a star used as an early standard mark.

Silver in its pure form is too soft for practical use. Through experimentation, the German goldsmiths evolved a process which combined pure silver with a very small amount of copper. The ideal proportions were discovered to be 925 parts pure silver to 75 parts copper. This mix has been in common use in Britain from the early 1200s to the present day, almost without interruption, and is referred to as sterling silver.[1]

In England, rigid legislation concerning the production of sterling silver has for hundreds of years provided a means of control by the Crown through a regulating body or guild known as The Worshipful Company of Goldsmiths and Silversmiths. The reason for this strict policing was dictated by the need to protect the 'coin of the realm': as money was made from solid silver until 1921 it was liable to debasement by unscrupulous people.

Severe punishment was meted out to those who chose to circumvent the law. It is recorded that in 1373 one Thomas Lauleye was put in a pillory with his counterfeit articles – in this case cups, hung around his neck – and then pelted with rotten fruit and vegetables. Those less fortunate were not only incarcerated in the pillory but also had their ears nailed to it.

In 1757 the death-penalty was introduced for those found guilty of imitating hallmarks. This was reduced to transportation to the colonies for a set period of 14 years in 1772. Few other industries ever had such extreme methods of quality control.

Heavy fines and imprisonment were, and still are, imposed against those caught in fraudulent practices, with the powerful Guild enjoying a similar status to the Inland Revenue in the UK or the American Internal Revenue Service. The regulating standards upheld by the Guild provided the basis for what was to become the finest silverware industry in the world. This reputation was founded not only on the quality of the metal used but also on design.

Although much silverware was produced for both ecclesiastical and domestic use prior to the 1700s, very little survives. Following on from the Dissolution of the Monasteries, the first great blow to English silver production, the expense of wars, even in recent times, has meant that silver plate was melted down and turned into coinage to pay the troops. Considerable quantities of early plate were lost in this way during the English Civil War. Nearer our own time, the First World War saw much of the tooling used to create beautiful pieces scrapped for the war effort. The cost of replacing these lost machines and tools, allied with changing social values, means that they will probably never be reproduced again.

The Restoration of the Monarchy in 1660 began a period of stability and economic growth as Britain expanded her Empire. The change was particularly beneficial for the silver trade following, as it did, the privations of the Civil War and the puritanical rule of Oliver Cromwell. The new monarch, Charles II, was a great patron of the arts and his subjects were only too glad to follow his lead and introduce ornament and decoration into their lives once more.

Another boost to the silver industry was the skill of the Huguenots, the French Protestants, who fled to England to escape religious persecution. Among the Huguenots were some of the best silversmiths of any era, renowned for their finesse and style. In Britain, it was often the case that a silversmith had great flair in designing a piece but lacked the skill to execute the design, and vice versa. Many of the Huguenot silversmiths possessed both these talents, achieving the highest recognition from the English Guild and training many apprentices, who in turn, became silversmiths of great repute. Silversmithing was also a notable exception to the guilds' tradition of banning aristocrats and women from their number; this lack of discrimination also aided the cause of artistry, as witnessed by the work of Hester Bateman and others.

The Industrial Revolution produced a new breed of silversmiths – the first industrial smiths. These men and women, usually self-made, combined the old art of silversmithing with new industrial machines and tools. The new methods brought together the greatest designers of the day with the most skilled craftworkers, each man or woman doing the job they knew best. This marriage of design and skill culminated in a continuity of manufacturing quality and artistry, previously a rarity. This was also the beginning of mass production, for better or for worse.

The combination of great silversmiths and designers, controlled quality, greater wealth and the emerging middle class, together with new styles and inspirations gleaned from the growing Empire, gave Britain its pre-eminence as the world's leading producer of fine silverware.

BRITANNIA STANDARD

This is a standard, higher in silver content than sterling, consisting of 958 parts silver to the thousand. It is softer and therefore less durable than sterling, although easier to work.

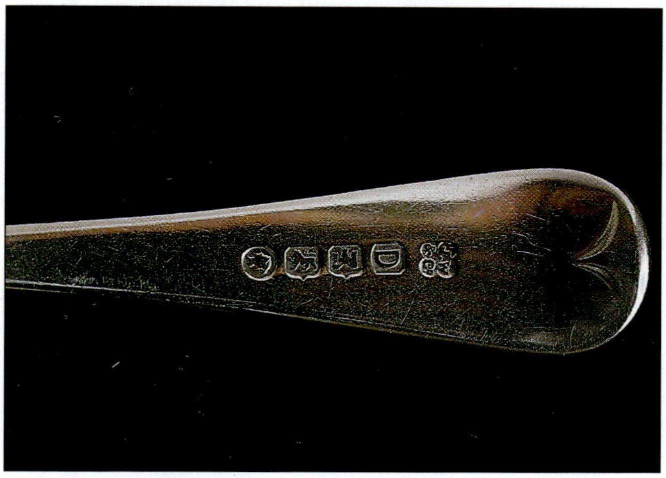

ABOVE
Exeter 1880

LEFT
The pseudo mark shown next to the real thing shows the differences between the two, the pseudo mark having no sterling mark (lion passant).

The Britannia standard was introduced by law and was the required standard between 1697 to 1720. Its purpose was to prevent the illegal clipping of coins, as the edges were frequently filed to use for making silver articles and the coin recirculated to trade at its face value. Often the coins would be melted down completely, creating a shortage.

Britannia is still acceptable as a silver standard today and its identifying symbols are used as shown below.

In America, no government or state control was ever exercized over craftsmen, purity standards of precious metals enforced or date stamps required. New York and Boston smiths created their own guilds, setting the standards for themselves and their colleagues. It can be supposed that the silversmiths of the other major cities formed similar societies. Baltimore actually had an assay office controlled by elected members, but this was a short-lived anomoly in United States silver history. Makers' names or monograms, and occasionally the place of manufacture or a number signifying the metal's purity, were the only identifying marks used. Of these, the only reliable means of identifying a piece of American silver is by means of the maker's mark.[2]

HALLMARKING

The primary reason for hallmarking, introduced in Britain in 1300, was and is still to guarantee the purity of silver and gold articles. Its system of marks serves to protect the public against forgeries and, in the past, was necessary to protect the debasement of coinage. Because the manufacture of gold and silver articles was allied with the minting of coinage made from these very same precious metals, a comprehensive system was established to test each and every piece made of gold and silver.

The testing or assaying procedure has always applied to not only the main body of the piece but also any part that can be detached from the main body by removing a pin or screw, such as handles, lids and finials. Once their authenticity is established these parts are hallmarked as well as the main piece, but often only with the sterling silver mark and, occasionally, the maker's mark. However, separate parts – such as the lid of an entrée dish – will be as fully hallmarked as the dish itself.

The 'Hall' referred to in the term 'hallmark' is Goldsmiths' Hall in London, governed by The Worshipful Company of Goldsmiths and Silversmiths. It has wielded great power under Royal Charter since the early 1300s and continues to control the industry today. Testing and marking is the activity of the Hall's main assay office, instituted in the mid 1400s, and other such offices in major British towns which were set up under the auspices of the company as the need grew.

AMERICAN SILVER MARKS

Unlike their British counterparts, North American smiths were not legally obliged to mark their goods with any details. Although many chose to put their names or initials on their work, dates and silver content were not recorded. Some makers stamped their silver with 'pseudo marks' such as a cartouche in the shape of a star, an eagle's head or an imitation of the British lion. As a rule, only the style allied with the maker's mark can be the guide to establishing the approximate date of American pieces.

An exception to this is silver from Baltimore, Maryland, the only city to establish an assay office, which operated briefly between 1814 and 1830. The symbol used to indicate a high percentage of silver was a liberty head, which was the town mark, accompanied by a date letter.

The silver content of 17th- and 18th-century pieces varied enormously. If made from melted coins the content depended on the country of origin, but if made from silver bullion the articles would be of sterling standard. After the War of Independence, the mint fixed a lower standard of 892 parts per 1,000 for American coinage manufacture. This was improved to 900 parts per 1,000 in 1837 and finally, in 1869, the sterling standard came into common use and goods were stamped 'sterling'. From the mid-1800s, until this improvement was adopted, it was usual practice to stamp goods with an indication of quality such as 'standard', 'C' or 'coin' (hand-hammered), 'quality' or 'premium'. This can be found on the back of spoons or along the rim or foot of tableware.

WHERE TO FIND HALLMARKS

Marks are sometimes hard to find. How and where they appear can also play a part in establishing whether or not an item is genuine. The following examples of where to look should prove helpful:

BELLS Near the lower rim either inside or outside.

BEAKERS Early beakers' marks are grouped on the base; up until the late-18th century they were marked in a line near the top edge.

BISCUIT BOXES Full marks should appear on the body, a lion passant and a maker's mark on the lid.

RIGHT

This Victorian coffee pot illustrates the hallmarking system whereby all detachable parts are marked separately. The handle can be removed from the main body by taking out the holding pins and the ivory heat insulators. The wing nut holding the finial screw can obviously be removed and so the finial itself is marked. The actual lid can be removed from the main body by taking out the hinge pin. The underside of the pot displays a full set of hallmarks. The detachable pieces are only marked with the sterling symbol and one other element of the hallmark.

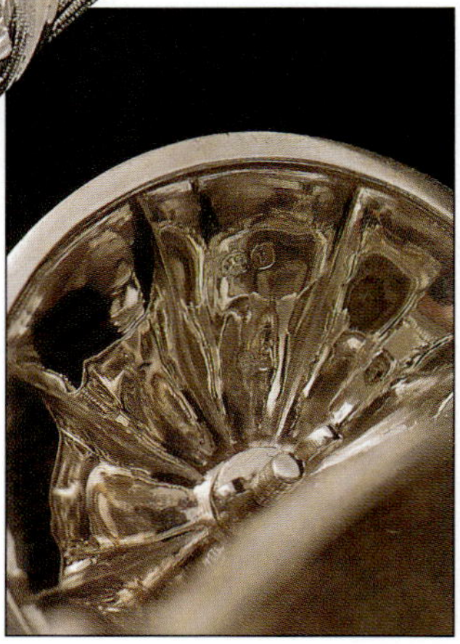

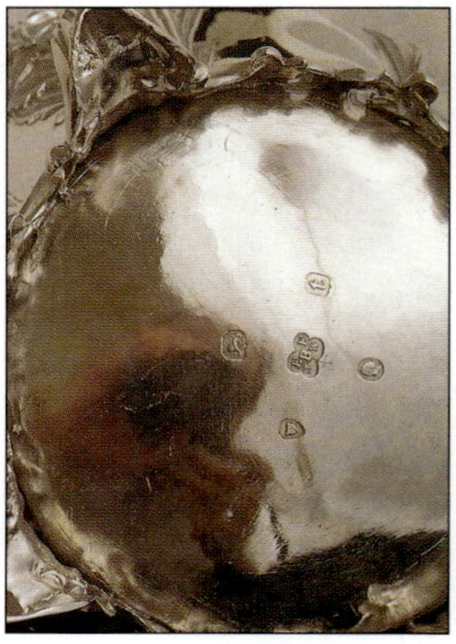

FAR RIGHT
Pair of silver and enamel salad servers. Despite the apparent similarities between both Liberty & Co. and the great artists of the Vienna Secession the authorship of this pair of servers is unknown. The spoon is stamped 'sterling' (right), suggesting they are of American origin. They show equally clearly the willingness to borrow from more than one source of inspiration in order to produce a really satisfying design.

BLEEDING BOWLS Either around the rim or in the centre of the base, inside or outside. The handle should have a lion passant mark. As these bowls were only made in England between 1625 and 1730, beware of any not of these dates.

BOXES Normally marked on the top as well as applying a full set to the base. Be cautious of boxes marked on the sides; the marks may have been let-in.

BUTTER SHELLS Marked under the plain grip or sometimes down one of the flutes.

CAKE BASKETS The handle, when present, should bear a lion passant mark, although there are some pre-1784 exceptions to this rule. Cake baskets were sometimes fashioned from soup tureen liners and in these cases the hallmarks will appear to be distorted.

CANDELABRA The same points as candlesticks apply to candelabra. All parts should be marked separately.

CANDLESTICKS Hallmark positions vary enormously depending on the date and style.

CAST STICKS Mainly marked underneath with one stamp on each corner or on the side of square examples, and in a line near the base on circular examples. Check pairs of cast candlesticks carefully as sometimes one of them is cast from the other. The copy will be very slightly smaller than the original and the marks will have a stippled appearance rather than a clean stamp. Occasionally candlesticks have been cast from earlier examples and re-hallmarked. This will be identified by its two sets of marks. (See also leaded sticks.)

CHAMBERSTICKS Up until 1720 these were usually marked on the topside of the tray in a straight or curved line. After this date they were marked underneath.

COASTERS The majority are hallmarked on the base. However, some made in the early- and late-18th century and the early-19th century were marked on the side of the body.

COFFEE POTS, CHOCOLATE POTS AND HOT WATER JUGS The main body should have a full set of marks scattered around the centre of the base, or in a straight line to the side. Lids should bear the lion passant and/or maker's mark as well as a duty mark when applicable.

Apart from let-in marks and later decorations, the most common pot and jug fakes are derived from tankards. As tankards tend to be shorter than pots or jugs, be suspicious if the item is squat. Another difference to note is that tankard lids have four or more marks whereas coffee pots have three or less.

CREAM JUGS These should always have the full set of marks. Ensure that you are not misled by a converted Christening mug with an added spout.

CRUETS Hallmarks should be present on all removeable parts. Note that prior to 1784, silver mounts on glass cruet bottles were not always hallmarked.

DINNER PLATES AND MEAT DISHES Early examples, prior to 1730, were marked on the outer raised rim between the bouge (inner border) and the outer border. On later examples the marks are in the same position but on the underside of the plate. Be wary of plates and dishes with hallmarks very close to the border or in the bouge.

ENTRÉE DISHES The marks usually appear in a straight line on the lid and are repeated again below the outside bottom to the side. They are rarely marked underneath the base. Detachable handles should have the maker's marks and lion passant plus the duty mark after 1784.

EPERGNES The stand and large basket should bear a full set of marks and the branches and smaller dishes should be marked with at least the lion passant and maker's mark.

FLATWARE/CUTLERY Each item should be stamped with a full set of marks except for some small items such as teaspoons, which may omit the town mark. Occasionally provincially made flatware will only show a maker's mark.

A common method of faking cutlery was to cast a copy of an earlier piece. As with candlesticks, cast fakes will be slightly smaller and the hallmark will have a stippled effect. To check if the whole set has been cast from one piece, look to see if all the marks are identically positioned. On a genuine set the marks would have been stamped by hand and therefore show irregular positioning.

GOBLETS Marked on the foot or the body.

INKSTANDS All detachable parts should have a maker's mark and a lion passant.

KETTLES Both the body and stand should be fully marked. All other detachable parts should be stamped with the lion passant and the maker's mark, with the exception of swing handles which are unmarked.

LEADED STICKS Usually marked in a line on one side of the base. Nozzles are usually marked although on some cast examples the marks were omitted or have been polished off.

If candlesticks are sold as a pair or set, make sure all the marks are matching. Candlesticks of different dates are worth between 10 per cent to 20 per cent less and those of different makers are worth between 40–50 per cent less.

MUSTARD POTS Should be hallmarked on the base or the body with full marks. The lid should be stamped with a maker's mark and lion passant.

PUNCH BOWLS As a general rule early bowls were marked on the side, 18th-century examples were marked underneath in a square formation and those made in the 19th century were marked on the side in a line. A common faking practice is to raise a bowl from a plate which results in distorted, oddly placed or upside-down marks.

SALT CELLARS Circular examples are marked underneath in a scattered pattern, although after 1790, a few examples were also marked on the side.

SALVERS AND TRAYS Should carry a full set of marks, normally in a straight line either on the top surface or the underside. Just like tankards, salvers and trays were often prone to alteration at a later date. Check to ensure the style is right for the year of manufacture.

SAUCE BOATS Marked underneath in a straight line. Boats with rolled feet are stamped on the foot itself.

SAUCE TUREENS The main body will be fully marked underneath, although those with pedestal feet have marks on the foot or the side. The lid will have full or half marks.

SOUP TUREENS Marked in the same manner as sauce tureens. Fakes are very rare but occasionally a tureen liner has had handles, feet and a lid added to it. In this case the main body will not have a complete set of marks.

STRAWBERRY DISHES Marked on the edge of the base or below the rim in a line. Sometimes they are made from dinner plates by hammering up the sides. This will produce thin edges and distorted marks.

SUGAR BOWLS Lids, if present, should have a full set of marks. Bowls or baskets with half a set of marks indicate they may have originally been epergne baskets.

TANKARDS AND MUGS No set rules for marking apply. As a guide, the bases were stamped until the 1770s, and on the body close to the handle thereafter. Tankards and mugs are often the victims of later chasing. This is quite easy to spot if you are familiar with the styles appropriate for different dates. If a spout has been added to make a cream jug, it must also be hallmarked to qualify as a legal alteration.

TEA CADDIES Look for full marks on the body, and the lion passant and the maker's mark on the lid.

TEA POTS See coffee pots. Fakes are very rare due to the abundance of genuine articles.

TEA URNS Full marks should appear on the body and the lion passant and maker's mark on removable pieces.

VINAIGRETTES Mostly Birmingham-made with marks on the base, lid and grille. Snuff boxes converted to vinaigrettes by the addition of a grille are easily detected because the fit will be poor.

WINE COASTERS Usually marked around the rim of the base. Cruet frames which have had the central handle and feet removed to change them into wine coasters can be detected easily by the marks left where the feet were positioned. This type of adaptation only occurs in single items, as pairs of cruets are rare and therefore more valuable in their original form.

WINE COOLERS Full hallmarks on the main body, usually on the base, but sometimes on the side. The liner and rim will also have all the marks with the exception of the town mark. The liners can be found with added handles to imitate a cooler but these will have incomplete marks, and no rim or liner.

WINE JUGS Display full marks on the body as well as the lion passant and maker's marks on the lid when applicable.

UNDERSTANDING HALLMARKS

The hallmarking system of impressing a number of symbols on articles of gold and silver is a very efficient method of quality control. Once the system has been understood, the marks are easy to decode. They show the place of origin, the identity of the maker, the year of manufacture and confirm the silver content.

The following tables give a comprehensive list of hallmarks by location, silver standard and year. A few maker's marks have been included by way of example – the full list of thousands would fill a volume several times the size of this book.*[3] The tables are repetitious. First establish the symbol for sterling silver – many assay offices use the lion passant – then find the date, represented by letters, using a different script for each alphabet cycle.

Next, look for the town or city mark and for any duty mark. The duty mark, a monarch's head, was introduced in 1784 and remained in constant use until 1889, although it has occasionally reappeared in recent times to celebrate a coronation year.

ABOVE
Birmingham 1907.

BELOW
Edinburgh 1815

BOTTOM
Britannia mark 1719 London.

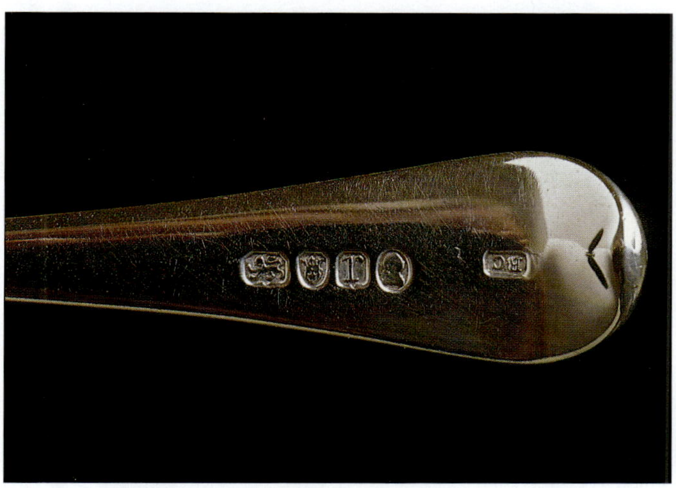

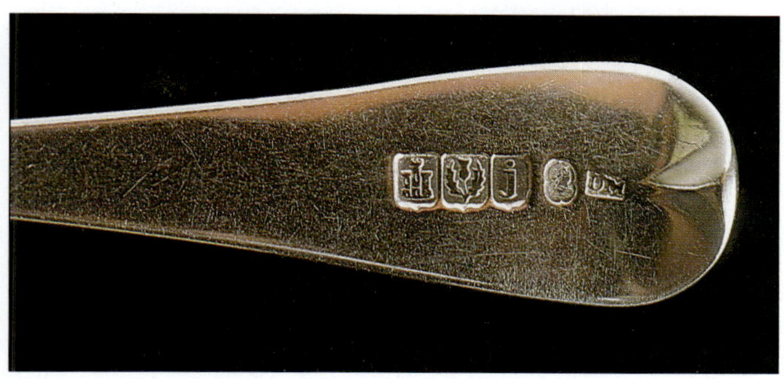

OPPOSITE
ABOVE LEFT
Silver bleeding bowl (porringer), London, 1683. This will be marked either on the rim or in the base.

ABOVE
The leopard is crowned, indicating the piece was made in 1792 and not 1832, which uses an uncrowned leopard (see table page 20).

TOP
Chester 1845.

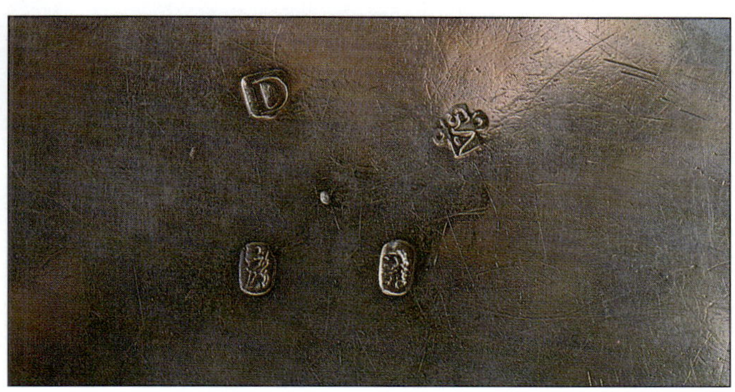

Dublin started using the mark in 1807 and Glasgow in 1819. Its purpose was to raise funds for the government to offset expensive war debts.

Modern additions to the hallmark system to look for are the Jubilee mark (1934–5) which commemorated the 25th wedding anniversary of George V and Queen Mary, the Coronation mark of Elizabeth II (1952–3) and the Queen's Silver Jubilee in 1977.

The shape of the shield surrounding each mark helpfully changed in tandem with every alphabet cycle and becomes easy to identify with only a little practice.

When examining your own pieces or those you wish to acquire, remember that only the main body will have a full set of hallmarks and that just the sterling silver mark and, perhaps, the maker's mark, will appear on detachable handles, spouts etc. Some Scottish pieces are only marked on the main body, so if a handle or finial looks incongruous it could be a later addition or not even silver (See Chapter 7). If in doubt, check the authenticity of the piece with an expert.

Spoons and forks made prior to 1770 are 'bottom marked', meaning that the hallmarks are placed close to the bowl or prongs along the shank. These marks look stretched and can be hard to read. A jeweller's 'loop' or magnifying glass, 8× or 10× power, is small enough to carry conveniently and strong enough to decipher these and other small marks.

[1] For a comprehensive and fascinating study see the new 'Jackson' published by the Antique Collectors Club in 1989, ed. Ian Pickford.

[2] Two recommended books on American marks are *The Encyclopedia of American Silver Manufacturing*, by Dorothy T Rainwater, useful for post-1820 sterling silver and electroplate, and *English, American and Foreign Silver*, by Seymour B Wyler, both published by Crown.

[3] *English Goldsmiths and their Marks* gives the most up-to-date list.

TOP

Dundee 1818. Double maker's mark (AC) on either side of the hallmark, date letter C, Scottish thistle and Dundee town mark. The Dundee assay office did not use the date letter on a regular basis.

BELOW LEFT

Glasgow 1841.

BOTTOM LEFT

Newcastle 1870.

ABOVE

Newcastle town mark (3 crowns) double duty stamp (monarch's head) sterling silver mark (lion passant) no date stamp, maker's mark. When the duty on silver was increased mid-year, a second monarch's head stamp was added. This was not a common occurrence, and suggests the piece was made *c.* 1788.

BELOW

Note that the queen's head is in an oval, showing us it is 1850 (date letter G) not 1874 which has the queen's head in a square with cut corners.

BOTTOM RIGHT

Next to the York town mark (lion within a cross) on the left is a smith's mark. The date letter indicates 1845.

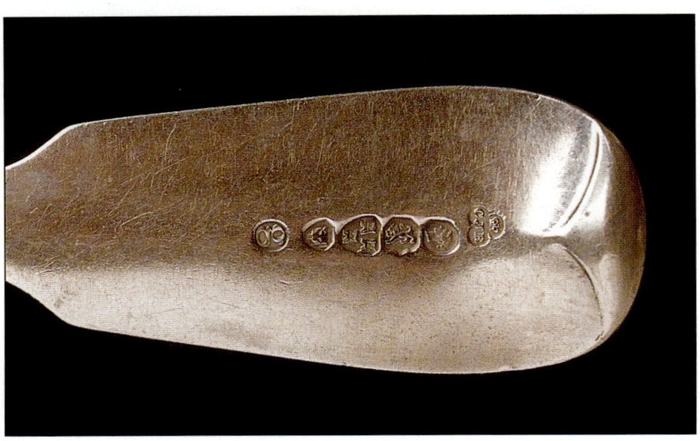

IMPORT MARKS

The Customs Act of 1842 made it illegal to import gold or silver ware into Great Britain and Ireland unless it had been assayed at a British office. In 1867 the foreign mark F was introduced as an addition to the British hallmarks. Pieces imported after 1904 were stamped with a symbol which replaced the F, denoting the decimal value of the standard used. (See hallmark table p 20).

Below: This Dutch snuff box, pierced basket and miniature chair all show the import mark F.
Bottom left: The basket shows the English hallmark of 1892 and the import mark F.
Below right: The snuff box shows the import mark F next to the date letter showing it was imported in 1896.
Bottom right: The miniature chair shows the date letter t for 1894 next to the import mark F.

HALLMARKS

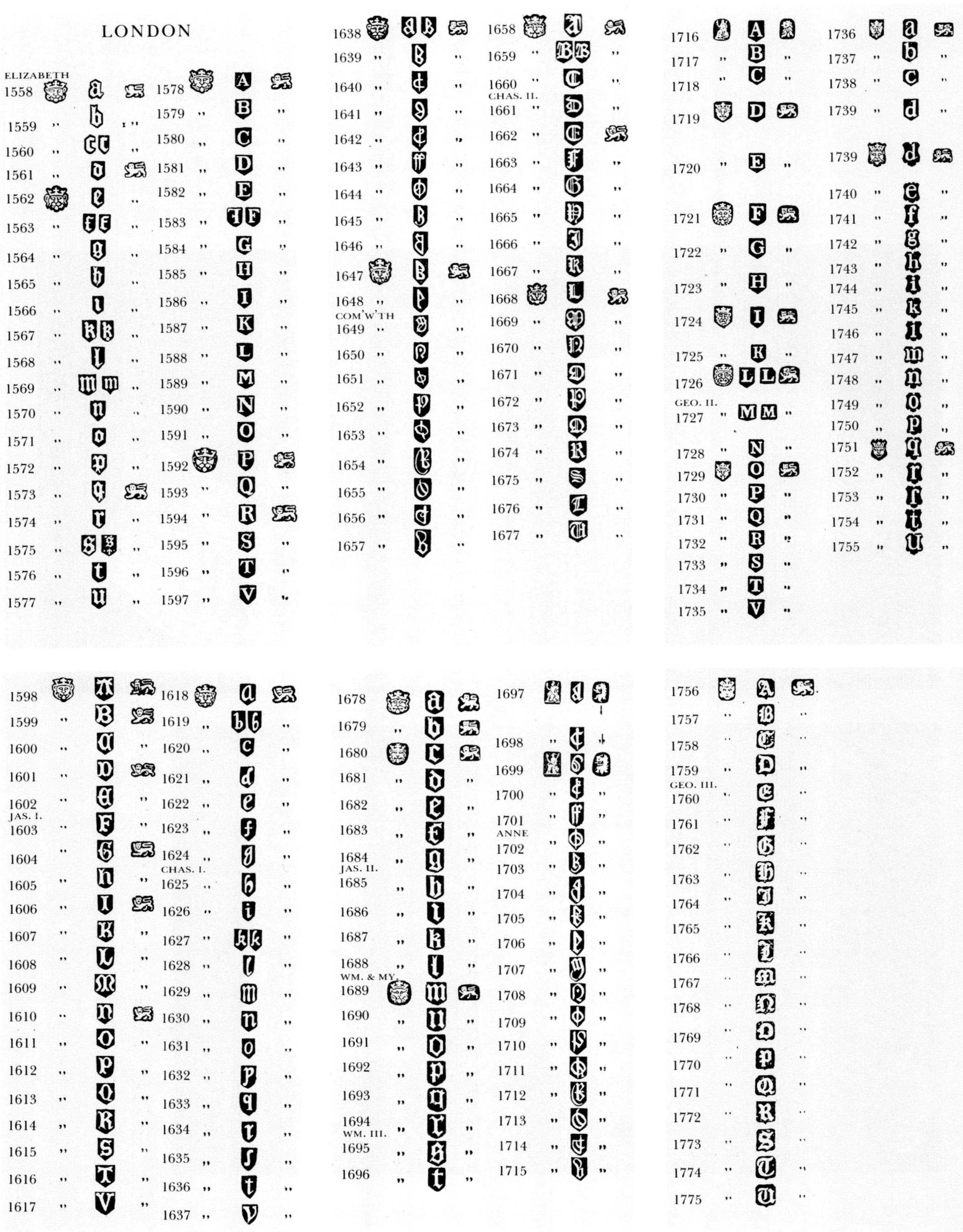
LONDON
ELIZABETH
1558
1559
1560
1561
1562
1563
1564
1565
1566
1567
1568
1569
1570
1571
1572
1573
1574
1575
1576
1577
1578
1579
1580
1581
1582
1583
1584
1585
1586
1587
1588
1589
1590
1591
1592
1593
1594
1595
1596
1597
1638
1639
1640
1641
1642
1643
1644
1645
1646
1647
1648
COM'W'TH
1649
1650
1651
1652
1653
1654
1655
1656
1657
1658
1659
1660
CHAS. II.
1661
1662
1663
1664
1665
1666
1667
1668
1669
1670
1671
1672
1673
1674
1675
1676
1677
1716
1717
1718
1719
1720
1721
1722
1723
1724
1725
1726
GEO. II.
1727
1728
1729
1730
1731
1732
1733
1734
1735
1736
1737
1738
1739
1739
1740
1741
1742
1743
1744
1745
1746
1747
1748
1749
1750
1751
1752
1753
1754
1755
1598
1599
1600
1601
1602
JAS. I.
1603
1604
1605
1606
1607
1608
1609
1610
1611
1612
1613
1614
1615
1616
1617
1618
1619
1620
1621
1622
1623
1624
CHAS. I.
1625
1626
1627
1628
1629
1630
1631
1632
1633
1634
1635
1636
1637
1678
1679
1680
1681
1682
1683
1684
JAS. II.
1685
1686
1687
1688
WM. & MY.
1689
1690
1691
1692
1693
1694
WM. III.
1695
1696
1697
1698
1699
1700
1701
ANNE
1702
1703
1704
1705
1706
1707
1708
1709
1710
1711
1712
1713
1714
1715
1756
1757
1758
1759
GEO. III.
1760
1761
1762
1763
1764
1765
1766
1767
1768
1769
1770
1771
1772
1773
1774
1775

1776		a		
1777	,,	b	,,	
1778	,,	c	,,	
1779	,,	d	,,	
1780	,,	e	,,	
1781	,,	f	,,	
1782	,,	g	,,	
1783	,,	h	,,	KING'S HEAD.
1784	,,	i	,,	
1785	,,	k	,,	,,
1786	,,	l	,,	
1787	,,	m	,,	,,
1788	,,	n	,,	,,
1789	,,	o	,,	,,
1790	,,	p	,,	,,
1791	,,	q	,,	,,
1792	,,	r	,,	,,
1793	,,	s	,,	,,
1794	,,	t	,,	,,
1795	,,	u	,,	,,

1796		A		
1797	,,	B	,,	,,
1798	,,	C	,,	,,
1799	,,	D	,,	,,
1800	,,	E	,,	,,
1801	,,	F	,,	,,
1802	,,	G	,,	,,
1803	,,	H	,,	,,
1804	,,	I	,,	,,
1805	,,	K	,,	,,
1806	,,	L	,,	,,
1807	,,	M	,,	,,
1808	,,	N	,,	,,
1809	,,	O	,,	,,
1810	,,	P	,,	,,
1811	,,	Q	,,	,,
1812	,,	R	,,	,,
1813	,,	S	,,	,,
1814	,,	T	,,	,,
1815	,,	U	,,	,,

1816		a		
1817	,,	b	,,	,,
1818	,,	c	,,	,,
1819	,,	d	,,	,,
GEO. IV. 1820	,,	e	,,	
1821		f		,,
1822	,,	g	,,	,,
1823	,,	h	,,	,,
1824	,,	i	,,	,,
1825	,,	k	,,	,,
1826	,,	l	,,	,,
1827	,,	m	,,	,,
1828	,,	n	,,	,,
1829	,,	o	,,	,,
WM. IV. 1830	,,	p	,,	,,
1831	,,	q	,,	
1832	,,	r	,,	,,
1833	,,	s	,,	,,
1834	,,	t	,,	,,
1835	,,	u	,,	,,

1836		A		
VICT. 1837	,,	B	,,	
1838	,,	C	,,	,,
1839	,,	D	,,	,,
1840	,,	E	,,	,,
1841	,,	F	,,	,,
1842	,,	G	,,	,,
1843	,,	H	,,	,,
1844	,,	I	,,	,,
1845	,,	K	,,	,,
1846	,,	L	,,	,,
1847	,,	M	,,	,,
1848	,,	N	,,	,,
1849	,,	O	,,	,,
1850	,,	P	,,	,,
1851	,,	Q	,,	,,
1852	,,	R	,,	,,
1853	,,	S	,,	,,
1854	,,	T	,,	,,
1855	,,	U	,,	,,

1856		a		
1857	,,	b	,,	,,
1858	,,	c	,,	,,
1859	,,	d	,,	,,
1860	,,	e	,,	,,
1861	,,	f	,,	,,
1862	,,	g	,,	,,
1863		h		,,
1864	Leopard's head as above	i	Lion passant as above	,,
1865	,,	k	,,	,,
1866	,,	l	,,	,,
1867	,,	m	,,	,,
1868	,,	n	,,	,,
1869	,,	o	,,	,,
1870	,,	p	,,	,,
1871	,,	q	,,	,,
1872	,,	r	,,	
1873	,,	s	,,	,,
1874	,,	t	,,	,,
1875	,,	u	,,	,,

1876		A		
1877	,,	B	,,	,,
1878	,,	C	,,	,,
1879	,,	D	,,	,,
1880	,,	E	,,	,,
1881	,,	F	,,	,,
1882	,,	G	,,	,,
1883	,,	H	,,	,,
1884	,,	I	,,	,,
1885	,,	K	,,	,,
1886	,,	L	,,	,,
1887	,,	M	,,	,,
1888	,,	N	,,	,,
1889	,,	O	,,	,,
1890	,,	P	,,	
1891	,,	Q	,,	
1892	,,	R	,,	
1893	,,	S	,,	
1894	,,	T	,,	
1895	,,	U	,,	

Year	Date letter
1896	a
1897	b
1898	c
1899	d
1900 EDW. VII.	e
1901	f
1902	g
1903	h
1904	i
1905	k
1906	l
1907	m
1908	n
1909 GEO. V.	o
1910	p
1911	q
1912	r
1913	s
1914	t
1915	u

Year	Date letter
1916	a
1917	b
1918	c
1919	d
1920	e
1921	f
1922	g
1923	h
1924	i
1925	k
1926	l
1927	m
1928	n
1929	o
1930	p
1931	q
1932	r
1933	s
1934	t
1935	u
1936	A
1937	B

Year	Date letter
1824	A
1825	B
1826	C
1827	D
1828	E
1829 WM. IV.	F
1830	G
1831	H
1832	I
1833	K
1834	L
1835	M
1836 VICT.	N
1837	O
1838	P
1839	Q
1840	R
1841	S
1842	T
1843	U
1844	V
1845	W
1846	X
1847	Y
1848	Z

Year	Date letter
1849	A
1850	B
1851	C
1852	D
1853	E
1854	F
1855	G
1856	H
1857	I
1858	J
1859	K
1860	L
1861	M
1862	N
1863	O
1864	P
1865	Q
1866	R
1867	S
1868	T
1869	U
1870	V
1971	W
1872	X
1873	Y
1874	Z

CHESTER

Year	Marks
c. 1683	RW, STER LING, RW
c. 1685	Sterl
1686–90	RW
1690–2	RW, PP
1692–4	PP, STER LING, STER LING
1695	BB, STER LING, BB, D
1696	E
1697	F

BIRMINGHAM

Year	Date letter
1773	A
1774	B
1775	C
1776	D
1777	E
1778	F
1779	G
1780	H
1781	I
1782	K
1783	L (KINGS HEAD)
1784	M
1785	N
1786	O
1787	P
1788	Q
1789	R
1790	S
1791	T
1792	U
1793	V
1794	W
1795	X
1796	Y
1797	Z

Year	Date letter
1798	a
1799	b
1800	c
1801	d
1802	e
1803	f
1804	g
1805	h
1806	i
1807	j
1808	k
1809	l
1810	m
1811	n
1812	o
1813	p
1814	q
1815	r
1816	s
1817	t
1818	u
1819 GEO. IV.	v
1820	w
1821	x
1822	y
1823	z

Year	Date letter
1875	a
1876	b
1877	c
1878	d
1879	e
1880	f
1881	g
1882	h
1883	i
1884	k
1885	l
1886	m
1887	n
1888	o
1889	p
1890	q
1891	r
1892	s
1893	t
1894	u
1895	v
1896	w
1897	x
1898	y
1899	z

Year	Date letter
1900	a
1901	b
1902	c
1903	d
1904	e
1905	f
1906	g
1907	h
1908	i
1909	k
1910	l
1911	m
1912	n
1913	o
1914	p
1915	q
1916	r
1917	s
1918	t
1919	u
1920	v
1921	w
1922	x
1923	y
1924	z

Year	Date letter
1701 ANNE	A
1702	B
1703	C
1704	D
1705	E
1706	F
1707	G
1708	H
1709	I
1710	K
1711	L
1712	M
1713 GEO. I.	N
1714	O
1715	P
1716	Q
1717	R
1718	S
1719 (LION PASSANT. LEOP'S HEAD CR.)	T
1720	U
1721	V
1722	W
1723	X
1724	Y
1725	Z

Year	Date letter
1726	A
1727 GEO. II.	B
1728	C
1729	D
1730	E
1731	F
1732	G
1733	H
1734	I
1735	K
1736	L
1737	M
1738	N
1739	O
1740	P
1741	Q
1742	R
1743	S
1744	T
1745	U
1746	V
1747	W
1748	X
1749	Y
1750	Z

Year	Marks	Date letter	Duty
1751		a	
1752	„ „ „	B or b	
1753	„ „ „	C	
1754	„ „ „	D or d	
1755	„ „ „	e	
1756	„ „ „	F or f	
1757	„ „ „	G	
1758	„ „ „	h	
1759 GEO. III	„ „ „	I or i	
1760	„ „ „	K or k	
1761	„ „ „	L or l	
1762	„ „ „	m	
1763	„ „ „	n	
1764	„ „ „	O	
1765	„ „ „	P	
1766	„ „ „	Q or q	
1767	„ „ „	R	
1768	„ „	S	
1769	„ „ „	T	
1771	„ „ „	U	
1772	„ „ „	V	
1773	„ „ „	W	
1774	„ „ „	X	
1775	„ „ „	Y	
1776		a	
1777	„ „ „	b	
1778	„ „ „	c	
1779		d	
1780	„ „ „	e	
1781	„ „ „	f	
1782	„ „ „	g	
1783	„ „ „	h	
	„ „ „	i	
1784		i	KING'S HEAD.
1785	„ „ „	k	„
1786	„ „ „	l	
1787	„ „ „	m	„
1788	„ „ „	n	„
1789	„ „ „	o	„
1790	„ „ „	p	„
1791	„ „ „	q	„
1792	„ „ „	r	„
1793	„ „ „	s	„
1794	„ „ „	t	„
1795	„ „ „	u	„
1796	„ „ „	v	„
1797		A	
1798	„ „ „	B	„
1799	„ „ „	C	„
1800	„ „	D	„
1801	„ „ „	E	„
1802	„ „ „	F	„
1803	„ „ „	G	„
1804	„ „ „	H	„
1805	„ „ „	I	„
1806	„ „ „	K	„
1807	„ „ „	L	„
1808	„ „ „	M	„
1809	„ „ „	N	„
1810	„ „ „	O	„
1811	„ „ „	P	„
1812	„ „ „	Q	„
1813	„ „ „	R	„
1814	„ „ „	S	„
1815	„ „ „	T	„
1816	„ „ „	U	„
1817	„ „ „	V	„
1818		A	
1819 GEO. IV.	„ „ „	B	„
1820	„ „ „	C	„
1821	„ „ „	D	„
1823	„ „	E	
1824	„ „ „	F	„
1825	„ „ „	G	„
1826	„ „ „	H	„
1827	„ „ „	I	„
1828	„ „ „	K	„
1829	„ „ „	L	„
WM. IV. 1830	„ „ „	M	„
1831	„ „ „	N	„
1832	„ „ „	O	„
1833	„ „ „	P	„
1834	„ „ „	Q	„
1835	„ „ „	R	
1836	„ „ „	S	„
VICT. 1837	„ „ „	T	„
1838	„ „ „	U	„
1839		A	
1840	„ „	B	„
1841	„ „	C	„
1842	„ „	D	„
1843	„ „	E	„
1844	„ „	F	„
1845	„ „	G	„
1846	„ „	H	„
1847	„ „	I	„
1848	„ „	K	„
1849	„ „	L	„
1850	„ „	M	„
1851	„ „	N	„
1852	„ „	O	„
1853	„ „	P	„
1854	„ „	Q	„
1855	„ „	R	„
1856	„ „	S	„
1857	„ „	T	„
1858	„ „	U	„
1859	„ „	V	„
1860	„ „	W	„
1861	„ „	X	„
1862	„ „	Y	„
1863	„ „	Z	„
1864		a	
1865	„ „	b	„
1866	„ „	c	„
1867	„ „	d	„
1868	„ „	e	„
1869	„ „	f	„
1870	„ „	g	„
1871	„ „	h	„
1872	„ „	i	„
1873	„ „	k	„
1874	„ „	l	„
1875	„ „	m	„
1876	„ „	n	„
1877	„ „	o	„
1878	„ „	p	„
1879	„ „	q	„
1880	„ „	r	„
1881	„ „	s	„
1882	„ „	t	„
1883	„ „	u	„
1884		A	
1885	„ „	B	„
1886	„ „	C	„
1887	„ „	D	„
1888	„ „	E	„
1889	„ „	F	„
1890	„ „	G	
1891	„ „	H	
1892	„ „	I	
1893	„ „	K	
1894	„ „	L	
1895	„ „	M	
1896	„ „	N	
1897	„ „	O	
1898	„ „	P	
1899	„ „	Q	
1900	„ „	R	
EDW. VII. 1901	„ „	A	
1902	„ „	B	
1903		C	
1904	„ „	D	
1905	„ „	E	
1906	„ „	F	
1907	„ „	G	
1908	„ „	H	
1909	„ „	I	
GEO. V. 1910	„ „	K	
1911	„ „	L	
1912	„ „	M	
1913	„ „	N	
1914	„ „	O	
1915	„ „	P	
1916	„ „	Q	
1917	„ „	R	
1918	„ „	S	
1919	„ „	T	
1920	„ „	U	
1921	„ „	V	

DUBLIN

Year	Date letter
CHAS. I.	
1638	A
1639	B
1640	C
1641	D
1642	E
1643	F
1644	G
1645	H
1646	I
1647	K
1648	L
COM'W'TH	
1649	M
1650	N
1651	O
1652	P
1653	Q
1654	R
1655	S
1656	T
1657	U
1658	a
1659	b
CHAS. II.	
1660	c
1661	d
1662	e
1663	f
1664	g
1665	h
1666	i
1667	k
1668	l
1669	m
1670	n
1671	o
1672	p
1673	q
1674	r
1675	s
1676	t
1677	u
1678	A
1679	B
1680	C
1681	D
1682	E
1683–4	F
JAS. II.	
1685–7	G
1688–93	H
	I
WM. III.	
1694–5	K
1696–8	L
1699	M
1700	N
1701	O
ANNE	
1702	P
1703	Q
1704–5	R
1706–7	S
1708–9	T
1710–11	U
1712–13	W
GEO. I.	
1714	X
1715	Y
1716	Z
1717	A
1718	B
1719	C, C
1720	A
1721	B
1722	C
1723	D
1724	E
1725	F
1726	G
GEO. II.	
1727	H
1728	I
1729	K
1730	L
1731	L
1732	M
1733	N
1734	O
1735	P
1736	Q
1737	R
1738	S
1739	T
1740	U
1741–2	W, W
1743–4	X
1745	Y
1746	Z
1747	A
1748	B
1749	C
1750	D
1751	E E
1752	F
1753	G
1754	H
1757	I
1758	K
1759	L
GEO. III.	
1760	M
1761	N
1762	O
1763	P
1764	Q
1765	R
1766	S
1767	T
1768	U
1769	W
1770	X
1771	Y
1772	Z
1773	A
1774	B
1775	C
1776	D
1777	E
1778	F
1779	G
1780	H
1781	I
1782	K
1783	L
1784	M
1785	N
1786	O
1787	P
1788	Q
1789	R
1790	S
1791	T
1792	U
1793	W
1794	X
1795	Y
1796	Z
1797	A
1798	B
1799	C
1800	D
1801	E
1802	F
1803	G
1804	H
1805	I
1806	K (KING'S HEAD)
1807	L
1808	M
1809	N N
1810	O O
1811	P
1812	Q
1813	R
1814	S
1815	T
1816	U
1817	W
1818	X
1819	Y
GEO. IV.	
1820	Z
1821	A
1822	B
1823	C
1824	D
1825	E E
1826	F
1827	G
1828	H
1829	I I
WM. IV.	
1830	K
1831	L
1832	M
1833	N N
1834	O O
1835	P P
1836	Q Q
VICT.	
1837	R R
1838	S
1839	T
1840	U U
1841	V
1842	W
1843	X
1844	Y
1845	Z

1846		a		
1847	„	b	„	„
1848	„	c	„	„
1849	„	d	„	„
1850	„	e	„	„
1851	„	f f	„	„
1852	„	g g	„	„
1853	„	h h	„	„
1854	„	i	„	„
1855	„	k	„	„
1856	„	l	„	„
1857	„	m	„	„
1858	„	n	„	„
1859	„	o	„	„
1860	„	p	„	„
1861	„	q	„	„
1862	„	r	„	„
1863	„	s	„	„
1864		t	„	„
1865	„	u	„	„
1866	„	v	„	„
1867	„	w	„	
1868	„	x	„	„
1869	„	y	„	„
1870	„	z	„	„

1871		A		
1872	„	B	„	„
1873	„	C	„	„
1874	„	D	„	„
1875	„	E	„	„
1876	„	F	„	„
1877	„	G	„	„
1878	„	H	„	„
1879	„	I	„	„
1880	„	K	„	„
1881	„	L	„	„
1882	„	M	„	„
1883	„	N	„	„
1884	„	O	„	„
1885	„	P	„	„
1886	„	Q	„	„
1887	„	R	„	„
1888	„	S	„	„
1889	„	T	„	„
1890	„	U	„	
1891	„	V	„	
1892	„	W	„	
1893	„	X	„	
1894	„	Y	„	
1895	„	Z	„	

1896		A	
1897	„	B	„
1898	„	C	„
1899	„	D	„
1900	„	E	„
EDW. VII. 1901	„	F	„
1902	„	G	„
1903		H	
1904	„	I	„
1905	„	K	„
1906	„	L	„
1907	„	M	„
1908	„	N	„
1909	„	O	„
GEO. V. 1910	„	P	„
1911	„	Q	„
1912	„	R	„
1913	„	S	„
1914	„	T	„
1915	„	U	„
1916		a	
1917	„	b	„
1918	„	c	„
1919	„	d	„
1920	„	e	„

EDINBURGH

1552		
1563	„	
c.1570	„	
1576		
1585	„	
1590		
1591	„	
1591–4	„	
1596	„	
1609	„	
1611		
	„	„
1617		
	„	„
	„	„
	„	„
c.1617	„	
1613–21		
1616–35	„	
	„	„
	„	„
1633		

1637		
1640		
1642	„	
1643		„
	„	„
1644	„	
1649	„	
	„	„
1651	„	
1660	„	
1665	„	
	„	
1669	„	
1674	„	„
1663–81	„	
1675	„	

1681			a
1682	„		b
1683	„	„	c
1684	„	„	d
1685	„	„	e
1686	„	„	f
1687	„	„	g
1688	„	„	h
WM. & MARY 1689	„	„	i
1690	„	„	k
1691	„	„	l
1692	„	„	m
1693	„	„	n
1694	„	„	o
WM. III. 1695	„	„	p
1696	„		q
1697	„	„	r
1698		„	s
1699	„	„	t
1700	„	„	v
1701	„	„	w
ANNE 1702	„	„	x
1703	„	„	y
1704	„	„	z

Year	Other marks	Date letter
1705		A
1706		B
1707	EP	C
1708		D
1709		E
1710		F
1711		G
1712		H
1713 GEO. I.		I
1714		K
1715		L
1716		M M
1717		N N
	EP	N
1718		O
1719		P P
	EP	P
1720		q
1721		R
1722		S
1723		T
1724		U
1725		V
1726 GEO. II.		W
1727		X
1728		Y
1729		Z
	AU	Z

Year	Other marks	Date letter
1780		A
1781		B
1782		C
1783		D
1784	KING'S HEAD	E
1785		F
1786		G
1788		H
1789		I J
1790		K
1791		L
1792		M
1793		N
1794		O
1795		P
1796		Q
1797		R
1798		S
1799		T
1800		U
1801		V
1802		W
1803		X
1804		Y
1805		Z

Year	Date letter
1857	A
1858	B
1859	C
1860	D
1861	E
1862	F
1863	G
1864	H
1865	I
1866	K
1867	L
1868	M
1869	N
1870	O
1871	P
1872	Q
1873	R
1874	S
1875	T
1876	U
1877	V
1878	W
1879	X
1880	Y
1881	Z

Year	Date letter
1882	a
1883	b
1884	c
1885	d
1886	e
1887	f
1888	g
1889	h
1890	i
1891	k
1892	l
1893	m
1894	n
1895	o
1896	p
1897	q
1898	r
1899	s
1900 EDW. VII.	t
1901	u
1902	v
1903	w
1904	x
1905	y
1906	z

Year	Other marks	Date letter
1730	AU	A
1731		B
1732		C
1733		D
1734		E
1735		F
1736		G
1737		H
1738		I
1739		K
1740	GED	L
1741		M
1742	EL	N
1743		O
1744	HG	P
1745		Q
1746		R
1747		S
1748		T
1749		U
1750		V
1751		W
1752		X
1753		Y
1754		Z

Year	Other marks	Date letter
1755	HG	A
1756		B
1757		C
1758		D
1759 GEO. III.	THISTLE	E
1760		F
1761		G
1762		H
1763		I
1764		K
1765		L
1766		M
1767		N
1768		O
1769		P
1770		Q
1771		R
1772		S
1773		T
1774		U
1775		V
1776		W
1777		X
1778		Y
1779		Z

Year	Date letter
1806	a
1807	b
1808	c
1809	d
1810	e
1811	f
1812	g
1813	h
1814	i
1815	j
1816	k
1817	l
1818	m
1819	n
GEO. IV. 1820	o
1821	p
1822	q
1823	r
1824	s
1825	t
1826	u
1827	v
1828	w
1829	x
WM. IV. 1830	y
1831	z

Year	Other marks	Date letter
1832		A
1833		B
1834		C
1835		D
1836		E
VICT. 1837		F
1838		G
1839		H
1840		I
1841	QUEEN'S HEAD	K
1842		L
1843		M
1844		N
1845		O
1846		P
1847		Q
1848		R
1849		S
1850		T
1851		U
1852		V
1853		W
1854		X
1855		Y
1856		Z

Year	Date letter
1907	A
1908	B
1909	C
GEO. V. 1910	D
1911	E
1912	F
1913	G
1914	H
1915	I
1916	K
1917	L
1918	M
1919	N
1920	O
1921	P

EXETER

c.1570
c.1571
c.1575
c.1580
c.1635
to
c.1675
c.1680
c.1690
c.1698

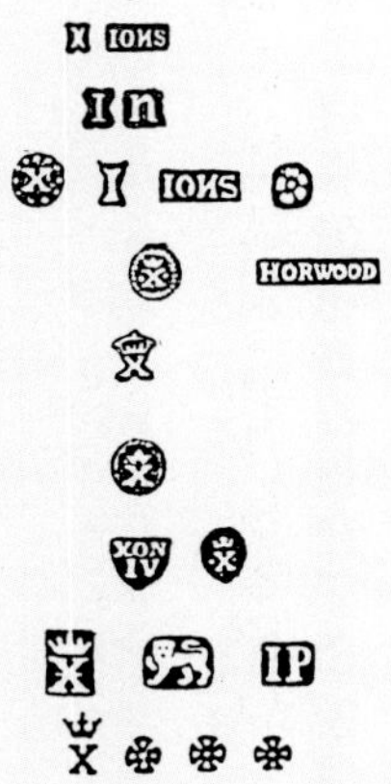

1701 ANNE				A
1702		„	„	B
1703		„	„	C
1704	„	„	„	D
1705	„	„	„	E
1706	„	„	„	F
1707	„	„	„	G
1708		„	„	H
1709		„	„	I
1710	„	„	„	K
1711	„	„	„	L
1712	„	„	„	M
1713 GEO. I.		„	„	N
1714	„	„	„	O
1715	„	„	„	P
1716	„	„	„	Q
1717	„	„	„	R
1718	„	„	„	S
1719	„	„	„	T
1720	„	„	„	V
1721				W
1722				X
1723	„	„	„	Y
1724	„	„	„	Z

1725				a
1726 GEO. II.	„	„	„	b
1727	„	„	„	c
1728	„	„	„	d
1729	„	„	„	e
1730	„	„	„	f
1731	„	„	„	g
1732	„	„	„	h
1733	„	„	„	i
1734	„	„	„	k
1735	„	„	„	l
1736	„	„	„	m
1737	„	„	„	n
1738	„	„	„	o
1739	„	„	„	p
1740	„	„	„	q
1741	„	„	„	r
1742	„	„	„	s
1743	„	„	„	t
1744	„	„	„	u
1745	„	„	„	w
1746	„	„	„	x
1747	„	„	„	y
1748	„	„	„	z

1749				A
1750	„	„	„	B
1751	„	„	„	C
1752	„	„	„	D
1753	„	„	„	E
1754	„	„	„	F
1755	„	„	„	G
1756	„	„	„	H
1757	„	„	„	I
1758	„	„	„	K
1759 GEO. III.	„	„	„	L
1760	„	„	„	M
1761	„	„	„	N
1762	„	„	„	O
1763	„	„	„	P
1764	„	„	„	Q
1765	„	„	„	R
1766	„	„	„	S
1767	„	„	„	T
1768	„	„	„	U
1769	„	„	„	W
1770	„	„	„	X
1771	„	„	„	Y
1772	„	„	„	Z

1773				A
1774	„	„	„	B
1775	„	„	„	C
1776	„	„	„	D
1777	„	„	„	E
1778	„			F
1779	„		„	G
1780	„		„	H
1781–2	„		„	I
1783	„	KING'S HEAD	„	K
1784	„		„	L
1785	„	„	„	M
1786	„		„	N
1787	„	„	„	O
1788	„	„	„	P
1789	„	„	„	q
1790	„	„	„	r
1791	„	„	„	f
1792	„	„	„	t
1793	„	„	„	u
1794	„	„	„	w
1795	„	„	„	X
1796	„	„	„	y

1797			A	
1798	„	„	B	„
1799	„	„	C	
1800	„	„	D	„
1801	„	„	E	„
1802	„	„	F	„
1803	„	„	G	„
1804	„	„	H	„
1805			I	„
1806	„	„	K	„
1807	„	„	L	„
1808	„	„	M	„
1809	„	„	N	„
1810	„	„	O	„
1811	„	„	P	„
1812	„	„	Q	„
1813	„	„	R	„
1814	„	„	S	„
1815	„	„	T	„
1816	„	„	U	„

1817			a	
1818	"	"	b	"
1819	"	"	c	"
GEO. IV. 1820	"	"	d	"
1821	"	"	e	"
1822	"	"	f	
1823	"	"	g	"
1824	"	"	h	"
1825	"	"	i	"
1826	"	"	k	"
1827	"	"	l	"
1828	"	"	m	"
1829	"	"	n	"
WM. IV. 1830	"	"	o	"
1831			p	
1832	"	"	q	"
1833			r	"
1834	"	"	s	
1835	"	"	t	"
1836	"	"	u	"

1857			A	
1858	"	"	B	"
1859	"	"	C	"
1860	"	"	D	"
1861	"	"	E	"
1862	"	"	F	"
1863	"	"	G	"
1864	"	"	H	"
1865	"	"	I	"
1866	"	"	K	"
1867	"	"	L	"
1868	"	"	M	"
1869	"	"	N	"
1870	"	"	O	"
1871	"	"	P	"
1872	"	"	Q	"
1873	"	"	R	"
1874	"	"	S	"
1875	"	"	T	"
1876	"	"	U	"
1877			A	
1878	"	"	B	"
1879	"	"	C	"
1880	"	"	D	"
1881	"	"	E	"
1882	"	"	F	"

1819			A	
GEO. IV 1820		"	B	"
1821	"	"	C	"
1822	"	"	D	"
1823	"	"	E	"
1824	"	"	F	"
1825	"	"	G	"
1826	"	"	H	"
1827	"	"	I	"
1828	"	"	J	"
1829	"	"	K	"
WM. IV. 1830	"	"	L	"
1831	"	"	M	"
1832	"	"	N	
1833	"	"	O	"
1834	"	"	P	"
1835	"	"	Q	"
1836	"	"	R	"
VICT. 1837	"	"	S	"
1838	"	"	T	"
1839	"	"	U	"
1840	"	"	V	"
1841	"	"	W	
1842	"	"	X	
1843	"	"	Y	
1844	"	"	Z	

1845			A	
1846	"	"	B	"
1847	"	"	C	"
1848	"	"	D	"
1849	"	"	E	"
1850	"	"	F	"
1851	"	"	G	"
1852	"	"	H	"
1853	"	"	I	"
1854	"	"	J	"
1855	"	"	K	"
1856	"	"	L	"
1857	"	"	M	"
1858	"	"	N	"
1859	"	"	O	"
1860	"	"	P	"
1861	"	"	Q	"
1862	"	"	R	"
1863	"	"	S	"
1864	"	"	T	"
1865	"	"	U	"
1866	"	"	V	"
1867	"	"	W	"
1868	"	"	X	"
1869	"	"	Y	"
1870	"	"	Z	"

VICT. 1837			A	
1838	"	"	B	
1839	"	"	C	
1840	"	"	D	"
1841		"	E	"
1842	"	"	F	"
1843		"	G	"
1844	"	"	H	"
1845	"	"	I	"
1846	"	"	K	"
1847	"	"	L	"
1848	"	"	M	"
1849	"	"	N	"
1850	"	"	O	"
1851	"	"	P	"
1852	"	"	Q	"
1853	"	"	R	"
1854	"	"	S	"
1855	"	"	T	"
1856	"	"	U	"

GLASGOW

1681		a
1683		c
1685	"	e
1689		i
1690	"	k
1694		n
1696	"	q
1698		s
1699		t
1700		u
1701	"	v
1704	" "	y
1705	"	z
1707		B
1709	"	D
1717		"
1728	"	S
1734	"	S
1743		S
1747		S
1756	"	S
1757		
1758		S
1763		E
1773	S	S
1776		O
1783		S
1785		S
1790		S
1811		

1871			A	
1872	"	"	B	"
1873	"	"	C	"
1874	"	"	D	"
1875	"	"	E	"
1876	"	"	F	"
1877	"	"	G	"
1878	"	"	H	"
1879	"	"	I	"
1880	"	"	J	"
1881	"	"	K	"
1882	"	"	L	"
1883	"	"	M	"
1884	"	"	N	"
1885	"	"	O	"
1886	"	"	P	"
1887	"	"	Q	"
1888	"	"	R	"
1889	"	"	S	"
1890	"	"	T	
1891	"	"	U	
1892	"	"	V	
1893	"	"	W	
1894	"	"	X	
1895	"	"	Y	
1896	"	"	Z	

1897				A
1898	"	"		B
1899	"	"		C
1900	"	"		D
EDW. VII. 1901	"	"		E
1902	"	"		F
1903	"	"		G
1904	"	"		H
1905	"	"		I
1906	"	"		J
1907	"	"		K
1908	"	"		L
1909	"	"		M
GEO. V. 1910	"	"		N
1911	"	"		O
1912	"	'		P
1913	"	"		Q
1914	"	"		R
1915	"	"	"	S
1916	"	"	"	T
1917	"	"	"	U
1918	"	"	"	V
1919	"	"	"	W
1920	"	"	"	X
1921	"	"	"	Y

1721				a
1722			"	B
1723	"		"	C
1724	"	"	"	D
1725				E
1726	"	"	"	F
GEO. II 1727		"		G
1728	"		"	H
1729	"	"	"	I
1730	"	"	"	K
1731	"	"	"	L
1732	"	"	"	M
1733	"	"	"	N
1734	"	"	"	O
1735	"	"	"	P
1736	"	"	"	Q
1737	"	"	"	R
1738	"	"	"	S
1739	"	"	"	T

1759				A	
GEO. III. 1760–8	"	"	"	B	
1769	"		"	C	
1770		"		D	
1771	"	"	"	E	
1772		"	"	F	
1773	"	"	"	G	
1774	"	"	"	H	
1775	"	"	"	I	
1776	"	"	"	K	
1777	"	"	"	L	
1778	"	"	"	M	
1779	"			N	
1780	"	"	"	O	
1781	"	"	"	P	
1782	"	"	"	Q	
1783	"	"	"	R	
1784	"	"	"	S	
1785	"	"	"	T	"
1786	"	"	"	U	
1787	"			W	"
1788	"		"	X	"
1789	"	"	"	Y	"
1790	"	"	"	Z	"

NEWCASTLE

c.1658				
c.1672		"	"	
c.1685				
c.1700				

ANNE 1702				A
1703	"	"	"	B
1704	"	"	"	C
1705	"	"	"	D
1706	"	"	"	E
1707		"	"	F
1708	"	"	"	G
1709	"	"	"	"
1712				K
GEO. I. 1714		"	"	M
1717	"	"	"	P
1718	"	"	"	Q
1719	"	"	"	D
1720	"	"	"	E

1740				A
1741	"	"	"	B
1742	"	"	"	C
1743	"	"	"	D
1744	"	"	"	E
1745	"	"		F
1746				G
1747	"	"	"	H
1748	"	"	"	I
1749	"	"	"	K
1750	"			L
1751	"	"	"	M
1752	"	"	"	N
1753	"	"	"	O
1754	"	"	"	P
1755	"	"	"	Q
1756	"	"	"	R
1757		"		S
1758				T

1791					A
1792	"	"	"	"	B
1793	"	"	"	"	C
1794	"	"	"	"	D
1795	"	"	"	"	E
1796	"	"	"	"	F
1797	"	"	"		G
1798	"	"	"	"	H
1799	"	"	"	"	I
1800					K
1801	"	"	"	"	L
1802	"	"	"	"	M
1803		"	·		N
1804	"	"	"	"	O
1805	"	"	"	"	P
1806	"	"	"	"	Q
1807	"	"	"	"	R
1808	"	"	"	"	S
1809					T
1810	"	"	"	"	U
1811	"	"	"	"	W
1812	"	"	"	"	X
1813	"	"	"	"	Y
1814	"	"	"	"	Z

1815	A				
1816	B	„	„	„	„
1817	C	„	„	„	„
1818	D	„	„	„	„
1819 GEO. IV	E	„	„	„	„
1820	F	„	„	„	„
1821	G		„	„	„
1822	H	„	„	„	„
1823	I	„	„	„	„
1824	K	„	„	„	„
1825	L	„	„	„	„
1826	M	„	„		„
1827	N	„	„	„	„
1828	O	„	„	„	„
1829 WM. IV.	P	„	„	„	„
1830	Q	„	„	„	„
1831	R	„	„	„	„
1832	S		„	„	„
1833	T	„	„	„	
1834	U	„	„	„	„
1835	W	„	„	„	„
1836	X		„	„	„
VICT. 1837	Y		„	„	„
1838	Z	„	„	„	„

1839					A
1840	„	„	„	„	B
1841		„	„	„	C
1842	„	„	„	„	D
1843	„	„	„	„	E
1844	„	„	„	„	F
1845	„	„	„	„	G
1846	„				H
1847	„	„	„	„	I
1848	„	„	„	„	J
1849	„	„	„	„	K
1850	„	„	„	„	L
1851	„	„	„	„	M
1852	„	„	„	„	N
1853	„	„	„	„	O
1854	„	„	„	„	P
1855	„	„	„	„	Q
1856	„	„	„	„	R
1857	„	„	„	„	S
1858	„	„	„	„	T
1859	„	„	„	„	U
1860	„	„	„	„	W
1861	„	„	„	„	X
1862	„	„	„	„	Y
1863	„	„	„	„	Z

1864	a
1865	b
1866	c
1867	d
1868	e
1869	f
1870	g
1871	h
1872	i
1873	k
1874	l
1875	m
1876	n
1877	o
1878	p
1879	q
1880	r
1881	s
1882	t
1883	u

NORWICH

1565		A
1566	„	B
1567		C
1568		D
1569		E
1570		F
1571		H
1573	„	I
1574	„	K
1579		P
c.1590		
c.1595		
c.1600		
c.1610		
c.1620		

1624			A
1925	„	„	B
1626		„	C
1627	„	„	D
1628		„	E
1629			F
1630	„		G
1631			H
1632	„	„	I
1633	„	„	K
1634	„	„	L
1635			M
1636			N
1637			O
1638	„	„	P
1639			Q
1640	„	„	R
1641	„	„	S
1642	„	„	T
1643			V

c.1645				
c.1650				AH
c.1655				AH
c.1660				AH
c.1665				WF
c.1670				AH
c.1675				TH
c.1680				MH
c.1685			TH	
1688			a	
1689			b	
1691			d	
1696			I	
1697				

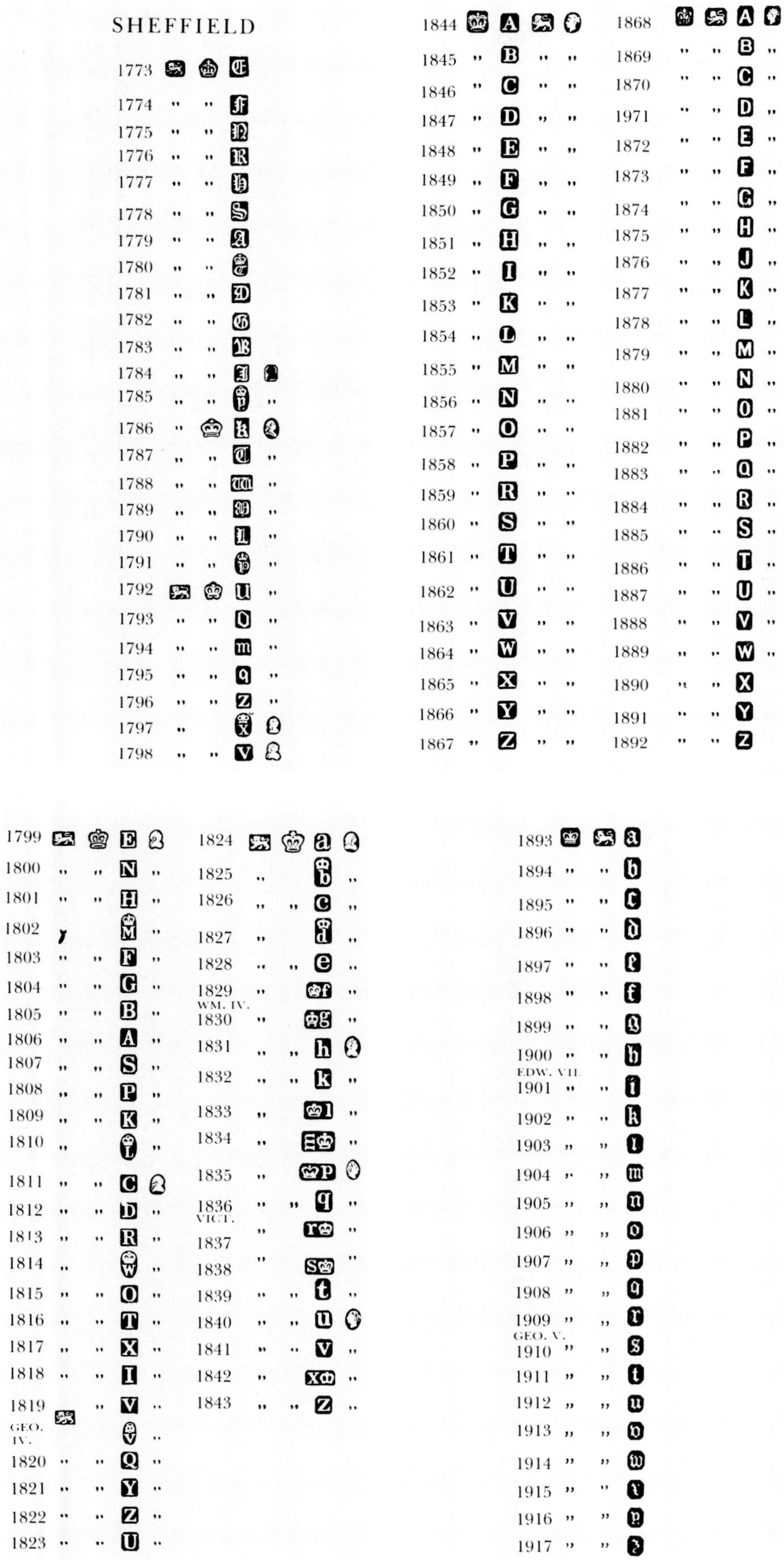
SHEFFIELD
1773 1774 1775 1776 1777 1778 1779 1780 1781 1782 1783 1784 1785 1786 1787 1788 1789 1790 1791 1792 1793 1794 1795 1796 1797 1798
1844 1845 1846 1847 1848 1849 1850 1851 1852 1853 1854 1855 1856 1857 1858 1859 1860 1861 1862 1863 1864 1865 1866 1867
1868 1869 1870 1971 1872 1873 1874 1875 1876 1877 1878 1879 1880 1881 1882 1883 1884 1885 1886 1887 1888 1889 1890 1891 1892
1799 1800 1801 1802 1803 1804 1805 1806 1807 1808 1809 1810 1811 1812 1813 1814 1815 1816 1817 1818 1819
GEO. IV.
1820 1821 1822 1823
1824 1825 1826 1827 1828 1829
WM. IV.
1830 1831 1832 1833 1834 1835 1836
VICT.
1837 1838 1839 1840 1841 1842 1843
1893 1894 1895 1896 1897 1898 1899 1900
EDW. VII.
1901 1902 1903 1904 1905 1906 1907 1908 1909
GEO. V.
1910 1911 1912 1913 1914 1915 1916 1917

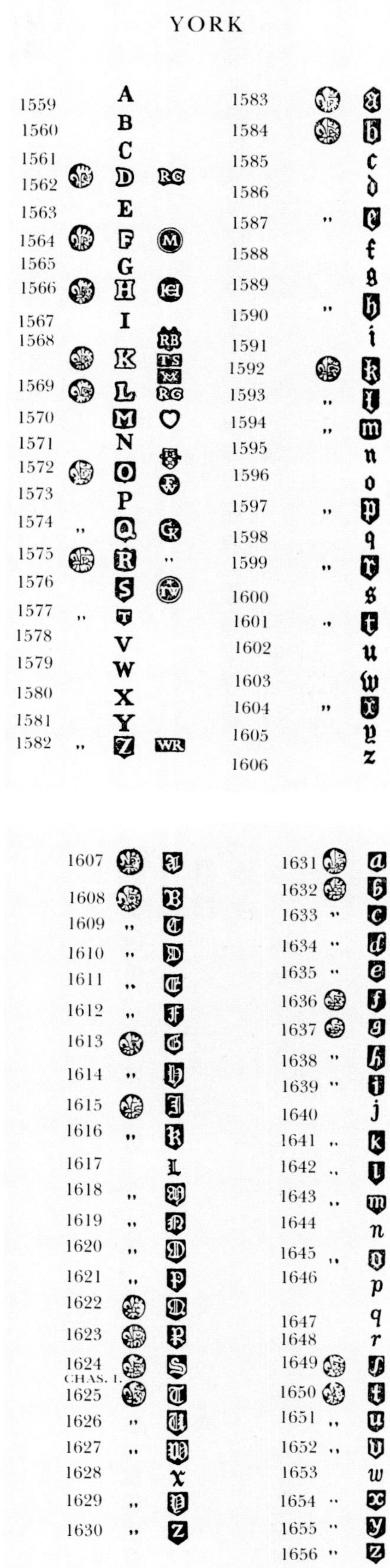
YORK
1559 1560 1561 1562 1563 1564 1565 1566 1567 1568 1569 1570 1571 1572 1573 1574 1575 1576 1577 1578 1579 1580 1581 1582
1583 1584 1585 1586 1587 1588 1589 1590 1591 1592 1593 1594 1595 1596 1597 1598 1599 1600 1601 1602 1603 1604 1605 1606
1607 1608 1609 1610 1611 1612 1613 1614 1615 1616 1617 1618 1619 1620 1621 1622 1623 1624
CHAS. I.
1625 1626 1627 1628 1629 1630
1631 1632 1633 1634 1635 1636 1637 1638 1639 1640 1641 1642 1643 1644 1645 1646 1647 1648 1649 1650 1651 1652 1653 1654 1655 1656

Year	Marks	Letter
1657		A
1658		B
1659		C
CHAS. II. 1660	"	D
1661	"	E
1662		F
1663		G
1664	"	H
1665	"	I
1666		K
1667	"	L
1668	"	M
1669	"	N
1670		O
1671	"	P
1672		Q
1673	"	R
1674	"	S
1675	"	T
1676	"	U
1677	"	V
1678	"	W
1679		X
1680	"	Y
1681	"	Z

Year	Marks	Letter
1682		A
1683	"	B
1684		C
JAS. II. 1685		D
1686	"	E
1687	"	F
1688	"	G
WM. & MY. 1689	"	H
1690		I
1691		K
1692	"	L
1693	"	M
1694		N
1695		O
WM. III. 1696	"	P
1697	"	Q
1698	"	R
1699		S

Year	Marks				Letter
1787					A
1788					b
1789	"	"	"	"	C
1790	"	"	"	"	d
1791	"	"	"	"	e
1792					f
1793	"	"	"	"	g
1794					h
1795	"	"	"	"	i
1796	"	"	"		k
1797					1 or L
1798	"	"	"	"	M
1799	"	"	"	"	N
1800	"	"	"	"	O
1801	"	"	"	"	P
1802	"	"	"	"	Q
1803	"	"	"	"	R
1804	"	"	"	"	S
1805	"	"	"	"	T
1806					U
1807	"	"	"	"	V
1808		"	"	"	W
1809		"	"	"	X
1810	"	"	"	"	Y
1811					Z

Year	Marks				Letter
Vict. 1837					A
1838	"	"	"	"	B
1839	"	"	"	"	C
1840	"	"	"		D
1841	"	"	"	"	E
1842	"	"	"	"	F
1843	"	"	"	"	G
1844	"	"	"	"	H
1845	"	"	"	"	I
1846					K
1847	"	"	"	"	L
1848	"	"		"	M
1849	"	"		"	N
1850	"	"		"	O
1851					P
1852					Q
1853					R
1854					S
1855					T
1856	"	"		"	V

Year	Marks			Letter	
1700				A	
1701				B	
ANNE 1702	"	"	"	C	
1703	"	"	"	D	
1705	"	"	"	F	
1706	"	"	"	G	
1708	"	"	"	I	
1711	"	"	"	Q	
1713	"	"	"	S	
1776				A	
1777				B	
1778				C	
1779				D	
1780				E	
1781		"	"	F	
1782	"	"	"	G	
1783	"	"	"	H	
1784	"	"	"	I	
1785				K	
1786				L	

Year	Marks				Letter
1812					a
1813					b
1814					c
1815	"	"	"	"	d
1816					e
1817	"	"	"	"	f
1818	"	"	"	"	g
1819					h
GEO. IV. 1820		"	"	"	i
1821		"	"	"	k
1822					l
1823					m
1824	"	"	"	"	n
1825	"	"	"	"	o
1826		"	"	"	p
1827					q
1828	"	"	"	"	r
1829	"	"	"	"	s
WM. IV. 1830		"	"		t
1831		"	"	"	u
1832					v
1833					w
1834					x
1835					y
1836					z

AMERICAN SILVERSMITHS' MARKS

The following are included to give an indication of the smith marks used in the United States. For a comprehensive guide consult The Book of Old Silver, *Samual B Wyler, Crown, New York. One date refers to the period of activity, two to the birth and death of the craftsman.*

P·A RA PA

ADAMS, PYGAN
NEW LONDON, CONN 1712–1770

G·A G.Aiken G.Aiken G.AiKen AIKEN G.AIKEN

AIKEN, GEORGE
BALTIMORE, MD 1765–1832

S.AYRES·LEX.K.

AYRES, S
LEXINGTON, KY 1805

Babcock

BABCOCK, SAMUEL
MIDDLETOWN, CONN 1788–1857

BAILEY & CO.

BAILEY & CO
PHILADELPHIA, PA 1850

IH IH IH IH

HULL, JOHN
BOSTON, MASS 1624–1683

JACCARD & CO ST.LOUIS

JACCARD & COMPANY
ST LOUIS, MO 1850

S.K S.Kirk Kirk S·KIRK KIRK S.KIRK SAM.L KIRK

KIRK, SAMUEL
BALTIMORE, MD 1792–1872

I·KUCHER

KUCHER, JACOB
PHILADELPHIA, PA 1813

Lamothe Lamothe

LAMOTHE, PIERRE
NEW ORLEANS, LA 1822

I·LT I·LT ILT I·LETELIER LeTelier

LE TELIER, JOHN
PHILADELPHIA, PA 1770

PR PR PR REVERE ·REVERE REVERE ·REVERE

REVERE, PAUL
BOSTON, MASS 1735–1818

PR P.Revere P.REVERE

REVERE, PAUL, SR
BOSTON, MASS 1702–1754

PS PS

SYNG, PHILIP
PHILADELPHIA, PA 1703–1789

PS PS PS

SYNG, PHILIP, JR
PHILADELPHIA, PA 1676–1739

MANUFACTURERS MARKS

The following marks are reproduced from Encyclopedia of American Silver Manufacturers *by D. Rainwater.*

ADELPHI SILVER PLATE CO. N.Y.
(Quadruple Ware.)
STERLING SILVER
QUADRUPLE PLATE ADELPHI SILVER PLATE CO NEW-YORK
(Quadruple Plate.)
(Holloware.)
STERLING
CONNECTICUT PLATE CO
ADELPHI —o— SILVER COMPANY
THE NEW ENGLAND SILVER PLATE CO. QUADRUPLE

ADELPHI SILVER PLATE CO
NEW YORK, NY est. 1890

ALVIN
Long Life Plate
ALVIN PATENT
ALVIN STERLING
SHERWOOD SILVERPLATE
STEGOR SILVERPLATE

ALVIN CORPORATION
PROVIDENCE, RI est. 1886

Amston
STERLING
Amston
FINE SILVER PLATE

AMSTON SILVER CO, INC
MERIDEN, CT est. 1965

AURORA WARRANTED ESTABLISHED 1869
(On Best Grade.)
PROVIDENCE SILVER PLATE Co. QUADRUPLE PLATE
AURORA S.P.M'F'G CO.
QUADRUPLE PLATE AURORA S.P.MFG CO. WARRANTED
(Hollowware.)
1869
AURORA SILVER PLATE M'F'G. CO.
12 Dwt.
(Flatware.)

AURORA SILVER PLATE CO
AURORA, IL est. 1869

BACHRACH & FREEDMAN
NEW YORK, NY est. 1896

BAKER-MANCHESTER MFG CO
PROVIDENCE, RI est. 1914

BALTIMORE SILVERSMITHS MFG CO
BALTIMORE, MD est. 1903

B. S. C.

BARBOUR SILVER Co.
QUADRUPLE PLATE

BARBOUR SILVER CO
HARTFORD, CT est. 1892

(Sterling) (Silverplate)

BARKER BROS SILVER CO, INC
NEW YORK, NY est. 1934

E & J BASS
NEW YORK, NY est. 1890

WM BENS CO, INC
PROVIDENCE, RI est. 1915

(Sterling & silverplate)

(Silverplate)

BIRMINGHAM SILVER CO INC
YALESVILLE, CT est. 1932

B S & F
Black Starr
Black, Starr & Frost Ltd

BLACK, STARR & FROST, LTD
NEW YORK, NY est. 1962

(Nethersole Bracelets.)

R BLACKINTON & CO
NORTH ATTLEBORO, MA est. 1862

BUCK SILVER COMPANY
SALAMANCA, NY est. 1900

J. E. C. & CO.

J E CALDWELL & CO
PHILADELPHIA, PA est. 1839

ALBERT COLES & CO
NEW YORK, NY est. 1836

CONTINENTAL
E.P. N.S.
ULTRAPLATE

CONTINENTAL SILVER CO
NEW YORK, NY est. 1920

CRESCENT

CRESCENT S/W MFG CO, INC
PORT JERVIS, NY est. 1922

THE DANFORTH COMPANY
NEW MILFORD, CT est. 1935

DAVIS & GALT
PHILADELPHIA, PA est. 1893

(Pewter Holloware)

ALDEN
(Pewterware)

M & B
STERLING

DERBY SILVER CO
DERBY, CT est. 1873

D. & H.

DOMINICK & HAFF
NEWARK, NEW YORK est. 1872

DISCOVERY
(Discontinued.)
CROMWELL
WATTEAU

WM B DURGIN CO
PROVIDENCE, RI est. 1853

ELGIN PLATE
STAR CUTLERY CO TRIPLE PLATE
CHICAGO SILVER PLATE CO WARRANTED 1849 TRIPLE
ELGIN AMERICAN

ELGIN
TRIPLE 12

ELGIN AMERICAN MFG.CO
WARRANTED

On plated silver knives about 1898

HAVONE (Cigarette Cases)

EAM

ELGIN-AMERICAN M/CO
ELGIN, IL est. 1887

EL-SIL-CO
ESCO
ELGIN SILVERSMITH CO

(Sterling)

ELGIN SILVERSMITH CO, INC
NEW YORK, NY est. 1892

E. J G
E&Co LTD

ELLIS SILVER CO, INC
NEW YORK, NY est. 1900

J E ELLIS & CO
TORONTO, CANADA est. 1877

FEDERAL SILVER CO. E.P.C.
(On silverplate)
FESCO

FEDERAL SILVER COMPANY
NEW YORK, NY est. 1920

FISHEL NESSLER CO.,
184 Fifth Ave.,
NEW YORK.

F.N.&CO.

FISHEL, NESSLER & CO
NEW YORK, NY est. 1893

GALT & BRO, INC
WASHINGTON, DC est. 1802

SILVER ON COPPER
(Used since Jan. 1, 1947)

GOLDFEDER S/W CO, INC
YALESVILLE, CT est. 1932

STERLING

GORHAM
(Gold)

TRADE-MARK.
STERLING

GORHAM
(art bronzes)
(Bronze)

GORHAM MF'G Co

Martelé
950-1000 FINE

GORHAM
(Plated silver)

GMCo
E P
GORHAM ELMWOOD PLATE

GORHAM
EP

G M Co
E P

Athenic
STERLING
(Sterling silver)

GORHAM COPORATION
PROVIDENCE, RI est. 1815

HS
STERLING
TRADE MARK

HARTFORD STERLING CO QUADRUPLE PLATED
HARTFORD STERLING CO NICKEL SILVER

HS Co
Silvered

H.S.Co

HARTFORD STERLING CO
PHILADELPHIA, PA est. 1900

H H

M FRED HIRSCH CO, INC
JERSEY CITY, NJ est. 1920

H+E
XIV
STERLING INLAID
HOLMES & EDWARDS XIV
MEXICAN SILVER
AZTEC COIN METAL
HOLMES H EDWARDS

ROLLED PLATE, HOLMES & EDWARDS
INLAID
HE
ORIENTAL
HESCO
MEXICAN CRAIG
HOLMES & EDWARDS XIV
EDWARDS
E HOLMES & EDWARDS STERLING INLAID HE
B. S. CO.
XIV. HOLMES & EDWARDS
VIANDE
STRATFORD SILVER PLATE CO.
STRATFORD SILVER CO.
STRATFORD PLATE
E STERLING INLAID
E HOLMES & EDWARDS SILVER – INLAID HE
STRATFORD SILVER CO AXI
HOLMES & EDWARDS INLAID
STRATFORD SILVERPLATE
WALDO HE

HOLMES & EDWARDS SILVER CO
BRIDGEPORT, CT est. 1882

HOMAN & COMPANY
CINCINNATI

(Nickel Silver.)

RICHFIELD PLATE CO. QUADRUPLE
(Popular Price Goods.)

SICK-CALL

HOMAN & COMPANY
CINCINNATI

OUTFIT.
(Church Goods.)

QUADRUPLE PLATE HOMAN SILVER PLATE CO.
SPECIAL METAL
HOMAN MFG. COMPANY
MADE IN USA

State House Sterling

PRESTIGE ★ ★ ★ ★ PLATE
(Used since Feb. 4, 1944)

DISTINCTION
(Used since March 20, 1950)

HOMAN MANUFACTURING CO
CINCINNATI, OH est. 1847

OLD CONSTITUTION

J H HUTCHINSON & CO
PORTSMOUTH, NH est. 1891

INTERNATIONAL STERLING

INTERNATIONAL SILVER COMPANY

INTERNATIONAL STERLING

I S

INTERNATIONAL (W STERLING

INTERNATIONAL STERLING

Wilcox IS

INTERNATIONAL SILVER COMPANY

I.S.CO.

INTERNATIONAL SILVER CO.

INTERNATIONAL S. CO.

INTERNATIONAL

£ STERLING

I.S. CO.

INSICO

ROGERS STERLING

R. & B.

INTERNATIONAL SILVER COMPANY

LA PIERRE

WILCOX & EVERTSEN

INTERNATIONAL BSC STERLING

INTERNATIONAL SILVER CO
MERIDEN, CT est. 1898

K

Kent Silversmiths

KENT SILVERSMITHS
NEW YORK, NY est. 1936

AMERICAN BEAUTY

WM B KERR & CO
NEWARK, NJ est. 1855

K (On sterling silver)

SILVER PLATED K (On plated silver)

KS Keystoneware

KEYSTONE SILVER CO
PHILADELPHIA, PA est. 1914

	ASSAYER'S AND MAKER'S MARKS	
1815	K&S A	A
1816	G	GF
1817	K&S E	E
1818	K&S D	D
1819	KIRK & SMITH C	C
1820	KIRK & SMITH A	A OR B
1821	S.Kirk G	G
1822	F	F
1823	Kirk E	E
1824	S.Kirk C	D OR C
1825 1826 1827	no example	B A G

YEAR	ASSAYER'S AND MAKER'S MARKS	DOMINICAL LETTERS
1828	20.11 M'S F SAML KIRK	F OR E
1829	S.KIRK D	D
1830	S.KIRK KIRK	C

ASSAY MARKS AND DOMINICAL LETTERS WERE NOT USED AFTER 1830

1830 to 1846	SAML KIRK S.K S.K 11OZ S.K 11OZ 10.15 S.KIRK S.KIRK SAML KIRK 10.15
1846 to 1861	S.KIRK&SON 11OZ SK & SON S.KIRK & SON 1015
1861 to 1868	S.KIRK & SONS 1015 S.KIRK&SONS 11OZ
1868 to 1898	S KIRK & SON 925/1000
1880 to 1890	S.KIRK&SON *S.Kirk & Son* 11OZ

YEAR	KIRK'S MAKER'S MARKS
1896 to 1903 flatware	S.KIRK&SONCO 925/1000 S.KIRK& SON CO 925/1000
1903 to 1924 holloware	S.KIRK & SONCO 925 S.KIRK&SONCO. 925/1000
1907 to 1914 flatware	S.KIRK & SON CO 925/1000 S.KIRK&SONCO 925/1000

1903 to 1907 holloware	KIRKCO 925/1000 S KIRK&SONCO 925/1000 S KIRK& SONCO 925/1000 S.KIRK&SON CO
1925 to 1932 holloware	S.KIRK&SON INC. STERLING
1927 to 1961 flatware	PAT. S.KIRK & SON STERLING
1932 to 1961 flatware	S.KIRK & SON STERLING
1932 to 1961 holloware	S.KIRK & SON STERLING S.KIRK&SON STERLING
1959 to 1961 flatware	S.KIRK&SON STERLING

SAMUEL KIRK & SON, INC
BALTIMORE, MD est. 1815

WITCH

DANIEL LOW & CO
SALEM, MA est. 1867

MAJESTIC SILVER CO, INC
NEW YORK, NY est. 1930

MANCHESTER MFG CO
PROVIDENCE, RI est. 1922

MANCHESTER SILVER CO
PROVIDENCE, RI est. 1887

LYONS SILVER CO. QUADRUPLE PLATE

MANHATTAN S/PLATE CO
LYONS, NY est. 1847

TRADE MARK. Manning Bowman & Co.

MANNING, BOWMAN & CO
MERIDEN, CT est. 1866

MERRIMAN SILVER CO
ATTLEBORO, MA est. 1897

COLUMBIA
SUPERIOR

This trademark adopted about 1866.

MIDDLETOWN PLATE CO
MIDDLETOWN, CT est. 1864

NORBERT MFG CO
NEW YORK, NY est. 1950

OLD NEWBURY CRAFTERS, INC
NEWBURYPORT, MA est. 1916

ONEIDA SILVERSMITHS
SHERRILL, NY est. 1848

PAIRPOINT
FLAT 1880 WARE.
BEST
(Flatware.)

BRISTOL PLATE CO.

(Holloware.) TRADE MARK. *(Holloware.)*

(On Sheffield reproductions)

THE PAIRPOINT CORP
NEW BEDFORD, MA est. 1880

STERLING
TRADE MARK

PHELPS & CARY CO
NEW YORK, NY est. 1904

(On sterling silver) *(Quadruple Plate.)*

HAND HAMMERED

POOLE SILVER CO. TAUNTON, MASS. NICKEL SILVER

TRADEMARK
PEWTER by POOLE

(On plated silver)

BRISTOL SILVER CORP.
POOLE STERLING CO.

POOLE SILVER CO
TAUNTON, MA est. 1893

NARRANGANSETT
(Used on pewter)

QUAKER
VOGUE

(On silverplate; used since February 1926)

QUAKER SILVER CO, INC
NORTH ATTLEBORO, MA est. 1926

COVENANT
(On pewterware)

QUEEN CITY SILVER CO, INC
CINCINNATI, OH est. 1888

REDDALL & CO, INC
NEWARK, NJ est. 1896

(Registered July 29, 1890)
(On sterling silver)

Viking Brand

REED & BARTON
(Nickel Silver Flatware and Hollowware.)

GOLDYN-BRONZ
(On plated silver)

REED BARTON
TRADE MARK
(White Metal Hollowware.)

Trade Mark
Sterling

TRADE MARK
STERLING

REED & BARTON
(On pewter)

SILVER ARTISTS CO.

REED & BARTON
TAUNTON, MA est. 1837

CMR

(Used c. 1900-1926)

TRADE CMR MARK

(Present mark)

R&B TRADE MARK

(On sterling silver)

(Used before 1900)

CMR

(Flatware.)

(On plated silver)

CHAS M ROBBINS
ATTLEBORO, MA est. 1892

ROCKFORD S.P. CO 1875 WARRANTED 12 DWT.

CUSTOM NATIONAL CUTLERY CO SUPERIOR

CROWN GUILD WARRANTED 3

J. G STERLING

ROCKFORD SILVER PLATE CO

ROCKFORD SILVER P. CO QUADRUPLE

ROCKFORD S.P.CO

CROWN GUILD

ROCKFORD SILVER PLATE CO
ROCKFORD, IL est. 1875

★ ROGERS & BRO., A 1.
(Best Quality Flatware.)

R. & B.
(Second Quality Flatware.)

★ ROGERS & BROTHER,
(H. H. Knives.)

★ ROGERS & BROTHER, 12
(No. 12 Steel Knives.)

★ R & B
(Pearl Knives.)

ROGERS & BRO.—GERMAN SILVER
*(German Silver Flatware, **Unplated.**)*

MANOR PLATE
(on low priced line)

TRADE MARK ROGERS & BRO. TRIPLE PLATE PATENTED
(Holloware.)

ROGERS & BRO
WATERBURY, CT est. 1858

TRADE MARK 18 83

F.B. ROGERS SILVER CO 18 83 TAUNTON MASS. QUADRUPLE

BEACON SILVER CO QUADRUPLE TAUNTON, MASS.

TRADE MARK 18 83

F B ROGERS SILVER CO
TAUNTON, MA est. 1883

ROGERS & HAMILTON.

ROGERS & HAMILTON
(on regular grade)

ROGERS & HAMILTON. A 1.

ROGERS & HAMILTON 12

HAMILTON

HAMILTON.
(on finest grade)

ROGERS & HAMILTON CO
WATERBURY, CT est. 1886

ACORN

SIMEON L. & GEO. H. ROGERS CO.

S. L. & G. H. ROGERS CO.

S. L. & G. H. R. CO.

ROGERS

SIMEON L & GEO H ROGERS CO
HARTFORD, CT est. 1900

WM ROGERS

WILLIAM ROGERS
CONNECTICUT est. 1836

Rosenthal

ROSENTHAL USA LTD
NEW YORK, NY est. 1879

SB

SAART BROS COMPANY
ATTLEBORO, MA est. 1906

O·F·D
(On sterling)

O F DINGELDEIN ST LOUIS USA
(On silverplate)

ST LOUIS METALCRAFTS, INC
ST LOUIS, MO est. 1950

SCHOFIELD CO, INC
BALTIMORE, MD est. 1903

THE GREAT SEAL OF THE STATE OF CALIFORNIA EUREKA

SCHULZ & FISCHER
SAN FRANCISCO, CA est. 1868

C S P

S S P

ALASKA METAL
(Used since 1908)

SALEM SILVER PLATE
(First used in 1914)

CAMBRIDGE SILVER PLATE
(First used c. 1909)

FASHION SILVER PLATE

PARAGON

PARAGON EXTRA

HARMONY HOUSE PLATE
(made by R. Wallace & Co.)

SEARS ROEBUCK & CO
CHICAGO, IL est. 1908

S

GEORGE B SHARP
PHILADELPHIA, PA est. 1848

S

SMCo S SMC

SHEPARD MFG CO
MELROSE H'LANDS, MA est. 1892

S

SILVER ON COPPER

SHERIDAN SILVER CO, INC
TAUNTON, MA est. 1944

S S

GILBERT
(Old Mark.)

GEORGE W SHIEBLER & CO
NEW YORK, NY est. 1876

SHREVE, CRUMP & LOW CO, INC
BOSTON, MA est. 1888

"Griffon" TRADE MARK

A L SILBERSTEIN
NEW YORK, NY est. 1904

Wm ROGERS.

(Flatware.)

SIMPSON, HALL, MILLER & CO

SHM&Co

E P

MANUFACTURED AND PLATED BY SIMPSON HALL MILLER &CO. U.S.A.

Wm Rogers Eagle Brand

TRADE MARK Sterling

(Hollowware.)

AMERICAN SILVER PLATE CO. QUADRUPLE

(Cheaper Grade.)

AMERICAN SILVER PLATE CO.

SIMPSON, HALL, MILLER & CO
WALLINGFORD, CT est. 1895

TRADE MARK

LAWRENCE B SMITH CO
BOSTON, MA est. 1887

REGISTERED LONDON HALLMARK

S&C

SPAULDING & CO
CHICAGO, IL est. 1855

Norman Plate

S.&A.

STANLEY & AYLWARD, LTD
TORONTO, CANADA est. 1920

OLD STURBRIDGE VILLAGE OSV

HISTORIC NEWPORT REPRODUCTION

WILLIAMSBURG RESTORATION CW ®

STIEFF STERLING

CW

THE STIEFF COMPANY
BALTIMORE, MD est. 1892

Stone

SSS

Stone

STONE ASSOCIATES
GARDNER, MA est. 1901

STERLING TRADE MARK

THE TENNANT COMPANY
NEW YORK, NY est. c.1896

TRADE MARK

THE THOMAE CO
ATTLEBORO, MA est. 1920

TIFFANY,YOUNG & ELLIS
J.C.M
20
(Used 1850-52.)

TIFFANY & Co 271 BROADWAY

TIFFANY & Co 271 BROADWAY

TIFFANY & Co
•
G&W
(Grosjean & Woodward)

M
300

J.C.M.
323
(Used 1852-53.)

2
TIFFANY & Co.
M LATE M
TIFFANY,YOUNG & ELLIS
550 BROADWAY
720

TIFFANY & Co
6601
G&W • G&W
ENGLISH STERLING
925-1000
4
550 BROADWAY.N.Y

(Used 1854-55.)

TIFFANY & Co.
657
M M
2712
GOLD & SILVERSMITHS
550 BROADWAY

TIFFANY & Co.
295
M ENGLISH STERLING M
925-1000
•
550 BROADWAY
(Used 1854-70.)

TIFFANY & Co. UNION SQ.

TIFFANY & Co
1063
M
1100
UNION SQUARE

(Used 1870-75)

TIFFANY & Co
MAKERS
STERLING-SILVER
925-1000
M
(Used 1875-91.)

TIFFANY & Co
9074 MAKERS 7184
STERLING SILVER
925-1000
T
(Used 1891-1902.)

1893 World's Columbian Exposition Chicago.

1900 Exposition, Universelle, Paris.

1901 Pan-American Exposition, Buffalo.

TIFFANY & CO.
12345 MAKERS 67890
STERLING SILVER
925-1000
M

TIFFANY & Co
14786 MAKERS 5885
STERLING SILVER
925-1000
C

(Used since 1902.)

The figures at the right and left of the word "Makers" are the pattern and order numbers, and vary accordingly.

Mark in use 1902-07
TIFFANY & Co
14786 MAKERS 5885
STERLING SILVER
925-1000
C

Mark in use 1907-38
TIFFANY & Co
12345 MAKERS 67890
STERLING SILVER
925-1000
M

Present Mark in use since 1938
TIFFANY & Co
MAKERS
STERLING SILVER
12345
M

TIFFANY & CO.
1824
QUALITY 925-1000
M
5731
UNION SQUARE
10

TIFFANY & COMPY
M
136

The following marks were used on silverware made for International Expositions in addition to the usual one:

TIFFANY & CO, INC
NEW YORK, NY est. 1837

TUTTLE SILVER CO
BOSTON, MA est. 1915

TUTTLE
FINE STERLING
TUTTLE SILVERSMITHS

CC

HH

FR

DE

RMN

HT

JFK

LBJ

GRF

TUTTLE SILVERSMITHS
BOSTON, MA est. 1890

MADE AND GUARANTEED BY THE VAN BERGH S.P.CO. ROCHESTER, N.Y. U.S.A.

BRITANNIA METAL CO. MADE IN U.S.A.

TIMOTY TUTTLE
BOSTON, MA est. 1890

BRITANNIA METAL CO.

VAN BERGH ROCHESTER N.Y. SILVER PLATE CO.

BRITANNIA METAL CO.

VAN BERGH S/PLATE CO
ROCHESTER, NY est. 1892

VICTOR SILVER CO QUADRUPLE PLATE

VICTOR S. CO.

VICTOR SILVER CO
See INTERNATIONAL SILVER CO

WALLACE BROS SILVER CO. W QUADRUPLE PLATE

ESSEX SILVER CO.
ESSEX SILVER CO.
QUAD PLATE
(Silver plated britannia)

V-L QUADRUPLE PLATE

MADE AND PLATED BY
WALLACE BROS. SILVER CO.

WALLACE BROS SILVER CO
WALLINGFORD, CT est. 1875

WAL STERLIN

WALLACE STERLING

WALLACE STERLING

WALLACE SILVERSMITHS
WALLINGFORD, CT est. 1833

WARREN SILVER QUADRUPLE PLATE COMPANY
NEW YORK
(*Medium Grade Hollowware.*)

WARREN SILVER PLATE CO
NEW YORK, NY est. 1901

TRADE STERLING MARK

THE WATSON & BRIGGS CO
ATTLEBORO, MA est. 1934

STERLING 925 1000 TRADE MARK

(1879-1905)

TRADE MARK STERLING

STERLING

(1905-1929)

TRADE STERLING MARK

(1910-)

WATSON COMPANY
ATTLEBORO, MA est. 1874

STERLING W.S.Co. TRADE MARK

WAYNE SILVER CO
HONESDALE, PA est. 1895

H J WEBB & CO
SPRINGFIELD, MA est. 1896

WEBSTER COMPANY 925 STERLING

WEBSTER COMPANY 925/1000 STERLING

WEBSTER COMPANY
NORTH ATTLEBORO, MA est. 1869

EGW&S

STERLING 925/1000

QUADRUPLE PLATE E.G. WEBSTER & SON N.Y. HARD WHITE METAL

E G WEBSTER & SON
BROOKLYN, NY est. 1859

W

W·B MFG CO

POMPEIAN GOLD

THE WARNER SILVER CO.

TRADE W.B MFG.CO. MARK

FVFR DRY
(On salt & pepper sets)

AVON
(On sterling)

MAYFLOWER
(On pewter)

THE WEIDLICH BROS MFG CO
BRIDGEPORT, CT est. 1901

WEIDLICH S/SPOONCO
BRIDGEPORT, CT est. 1915

WCo

TRADE MARK

STERLING

WENDELL MFG COMPANY
CHICAGO, IL est. 1850

THE WESSELL SILVER CO
ΜΕΤΑΛΟΣ
TRADE MARK
SOLID WESSELL SILVER

THE WESSELL SILVER CO
NEW YORK, NY est. 1945

TRADE MARK

W

FRANK M WHITING CO
NORTH ATTLEBORO, MASS est. 1878

WHITNEY JEWELRY CO
BOSTON, MA est. 1883

WILCOX & EVERTSEN
NEW YORK, NY est. 1889

TRADE MARK

H C WILCOX & CO
MERIDEN, CT est. 1848

WILCOX S.P. CO
INTERNATIONAL S. CO.
SUPERIOR S.P.CO.
SUPERIOR EPNS S.P.CO.
WILCOX SILVER PLATE CO.
WILCOX S.P. CO. EPNS INTERNATIONAL S. CO

QUADRUPLE PLATE WILCOX SILVER PLATE CO. MERIDEN, CONN.
WILCOX SILVER PLATE
MADE & GUARANTEED BY WILCOX SILVER PLATE CO. USA
SUPERIOR SILVER CO

STERLING

PEWTER
BY
WILCOX
(Pewter Hollowware)

WILCOX SILVER PLATE CO
MERIDEN, CT est. 1865

TRADE MARK
STERLING

WILCOX & WAGONER
NEW YORK, NY est. 1904

WILEY-CRAWFORD CO, INC
NEWARK, NJ est. 1915

WILKINSON

WILKINSON SWORD CO
LONDON & SHEFFIELD est. 1909

Williams TRIPLE PLATE

WILLIAMS BROS MFG CO
NAUBUC, CT est. 1880

R & W

ROGER WILLIAMS SILVER CO
PROVIDENCE, RI est 1900

RWP® ARMETALE

WILTON BRASS FOUNDRY
COLUMBIA, PA

TRADE MARK

WOODSIDE STERLNG CO
NEW YORK, NY est. 1896

WORLD HAND FORGED

WORLD HAND FORGED MFG CO
NEW YORK, NY est. 1950

UNLETTERED TRADEMARKS

These symbols appear on silver articles without the company name, or any accompanying initial.

THOMAS G BROWN & SONS

THE MELROSE SILVER CO

TRADE MARK.

TORONTO SILVER PLATE CO

E G WEBSTER & SON

ALBANY S/PLATE CO

FENNIMAN CO

BEN SPIER

FRANKLIN S/PLATE CO

C F KEES & CO

G W PARKS COMPANY

PARKS BROS & ROGERS

WM KNOLL & CO

TH MARTHINSEN

J TOSTRUP

FINE ARTS S/SILVER CO

KENT & STANLEY CO, LTD

BROWN & WARD

MERMOD, JACCARD & KING JEWELERY CO

WILLIAM LINKER

JOSEPH MAYER & BROS

TOWLE SILVERSMITHS

INTERNATIONAL SILVER CO

MECHANICS SILVER CO & WATSON CO

C E BARKER MFG CO

JACK BOWLING

ALBERT FELDENHEIMER

MAX HIRSCH

LEHMAN BROS S/W CORP

S J LEVI & CO, LTD

H H CURTIS & CO

THE MAUSER MFG CO

REDLICH & CO

SACKETT & CO, LTD

THE MERRILL SHOPS

A L SILBERSTEIN

A L SILBERSTEIN

TILDEN-THURBER CO

THORNTON & CO

MAYO & CO

WILLIAM C FINCK CO

SHREVE, CRUMP & LOW CO, INC

HENRY C HASKELL

MAJESTIC SILVER CO

GENOVA SILVER CO, INC

MERIDEN BRITANNIA CO

J T INMAN & CO

J W ROSENBAUM & CO

COLONIAL SILVER CO, INC

HAWTHORNE MFG CO

CHARTER COMPANY

ECKFELDT & ACKLEY

LOTT & SCHMITT, INC

MATHEWS & PRIOR

HANLE & DEBLER, INC

PRILL SILVER CO, INC

GEBRUEDER NOELLE

NEW ORLEANS SILVERSMITHS

J J COHN

MEDALLIC ART CO

UTOPIAN SILVER DEPOSIT AND NOVELTY CO

ROGER WILLIAMS SILVER CO

AUG C FRANK CO, INC

R GLEASON & SONS

HARRIS & SCHAFER

ROMAN SILVERSMITHS, INC

SUTTON HOO JEWELERS

MONTGOMERY BROS

L KIMBALL & SON

H G HUDSON

MILLIE B LOGAN

E A BLISS CO

FERDINAND C LAMY

WILLIAM F NEWHALL

WILLIAM H SAXTON, JR

N G WOOD & SONS

H G HUDSON

MERIDEN BRITANNIA CO

THOMAS F BROGAN

BROWN & BROS

HERBST & WASSALL

HOWARD & COCKSHAW CO

J F FRADLEY & CO

ALBERT J GANNON

BASCH BROS & CO

DAY, CLARK & CO

M EISENSTADT JEWELRY CO

FUCHS & BEIDERHASE

SUTTON HOO JEWELERS

JAMES E BLAKE CO

THE BASSETT JEWELRY CO

TOWLE SILVERSMITHS

D C BOURQUIN

Old Sheffield Plate/Fused Plate

Considerable confusion is caused by the variety of words used to describe articles made from copper and then coated with silver by fusion, used mainly for domestic purposes. It is correctly known as Old Sheffield Plate or Fused Plate; the terms are interchangeable. However, Sheffield Plate, Silver Plate or Real Sheffield Plate are all terms misused, innocently or otherwise, by silver sellers and the public alike, to describe erroneously Old Sheffield or fused plate.

In Britain, prior to 1740, plate was the collective name for all articles of solid silver. They fell into the two categories – ecclesiastical and household plate. Many magnificent examples of mazers, chalices and other church paraphernalia have survived to this day. Household plate included candlesticks, chocolate pots, tobacco boxes, toilet sets, inkstands and all other functional and decorative objects for the home. When the

ABOVE

A selection of styles over 80 years showing the distinct change from one period to another – essential in helping to date Sheffield Plate as styles were not repeated. Far left: Corinthian column *c.* 1770. These Romanesque designs gave way to a much more delicate influence in the neo-classical style of the 1780s and 1790s. Second left: A typical neo-classical style candlestick of the 1780s, with its bellflower swags and delicate beading. Centre: With its tapering column and clean unfussy lines and gadroon borders, this typifies the years around 1800–1810. This in turn gives way to the more massive forms of the Regency period *c.* 1820. Second right: The characteristic overlapping acanthus leaves on a telescope Regency candlestick *c.* 1820. Far right: Produced around 1845, at the end of the Old Sheffield period, the bulbous fluted form typifies the beginning of the Victorian era.

LEFT

A pear-shaped coffee pot on spreading circular base *c.* 1765.

LEFT

A coffee pot of tapering oval form *c.* 1790 incorporating an applied band of bright cut engraving. This urn shape typifies the Grecian influence of the Adam period.

LEFT

A coffee jug of compressed pear form incorporating fluting and gadroon borders typical of articles made around 1800. The handles are usually of fruitwood. Sometimes woven wicker coverings, or even leather coverings are found on wooden or metal handles although not many have survived intact.

LEFT

A Victorian 'transitional' coffee pot of bulbous fluted form, sometimes referred to as the melon pattern, with hand chased cartouche and scrolling foliage *c.* 1840

fused process was introduced in 1742, its products became known as fused plate to distinguish this new unhallmarked 'silver' from sterling silver, which it resembled at a glance.

Sheffield was the birthplace and the centre of this new manufacturing industry which spread to Birmingham and to a lesser extent to Russia, France and other parts of Europe. As Britain had such a hold on the industry, no other country could compete with the quality of the British goods. Vast quantities were exported to Europe, especially France, prior to the Revolution and also to the Americas, which had no fused plate industry.

Manufacture by this process stopped completely by 1850 to be replaced by a new technique, electroplating. Because of the strong historical association with Sheffield, people started to refer to the defunct process of fusing plate as Old Sheffield Plate – and the name has stuck.

Manufacturers have in the past and still do stamp items – usually electroplate goods – with words that could imply association with the fused plate process. This may mislead the unwary. Sales staff and private individuals often use verbal descriptions with the same kind of implication. The reason is normally to attach greater importance to a piece, thereby exacting a higher price.

The Origins Of Old Sheffield Plate

The accidental invention of the fused plate process in 1742, was attributed to Thomas Boulsover, a Sheffield cutler, and later, button maker. It is said that Boulsover, while attempting to pour molten silver into a mould, spilt some of it onto his workbench. When he began to clear up the spillage, he noticed that some of the silver had splashed onto a copper knife haft and the two metals had fused together. Although this fortuitous event brought eventual recognition to Mr Boulsover, the financial rewards were reaped by others. It took roughly 10 years from its discovery for the process to be perfected and saleable goods produced.

However, it took much longer to gain acceptance from the rich and influential who, until the Industrial Revolution, had been almost the only ones able to afford more than the basic requirements of life. It was this comparatively small group that controlled and guided all aspects of life from foreign policy to fashion.

At first, as only the rich could afford silver household articles, the new process did not seem to have an immediate application. Why buy 'poor man's silver' as it was nicknamed, when you could have the real thing?

But a new market was developing. The invention of the steam engine, and the subsequent industrialization which followed, saw the emergence of a new social group with great purchasing power – middle class with aspirations to have a slice of the cake enjoyed by their betters. In America, the Revolution brought with it the demand, as well as the means to produce, large quantities of affordable product. Grand hotels which previously used sterling silver, and inns, which had used pewter, became substantial buyers of fused plate.

It is important to remember that silver articles were not purely ornamental but served a variety of essential, everyday purposes. It was only the cost of sterling silver that put it out of reach for most people. The new process – with its thin cover-

TOP LEFT

Salver from 1765 with punched copper border.

TOP RIGHT

An oval salver with applied fine bead pattern border *c.* 1790. No silver shield has been set in, therefore the engraved initials have exposed the copper beneath. These initials may have been done at a later date.

BOTTOM LEFT

Oblong salver with gadroon border resting on scroll supports *c.* 1800.

BOTTOM RIGHT

Salver with flat chased scroll work, foliage and floral decorations *c.* 1830. Notice the applied border picking up the same pattern.

TOP
Soup tureen and cover surmounted by a stag's head finial. The finial was almost certainly taken from the crest of the family which commissioned the soup tureen and would have been part of a complete table suite. The tureen has a let-in shield so that the crest could be engraved if required. The bulbous panel fluting, overlapping foliage, leaf scroll and shell border, indicate the tureen was made *c.* 1830.

ABOVE
An exceptional urn made in Sheffield *c.* 1830 typifying the period with its massive compressed circular body and highly ornamented hand-chased sections, as well as the overlapping acanthus leaf and shell mounts. Earlier examples would have appeared in 1800 with the same shape but without the majority of the ornamentation and a much simpler spiggot and finial.

ing of sterling over a core of copper – cut down the cost dramatically.

As a result, over the next hundred years, every conceivable article that had previously been made in silver was copied using this new method. At first the main customers were the middle and professional classes. But in the 1780s, the cost of sterling silver rose sharply and a tax was levied on each article produced, to raise funds for Britain's overseas obligations, particularly for enacting the programme for American Independence and new systems for Ireland and India. This, and the perfection of the fused plate process, led the gentry finally to accept that silver-plated goods had a place in their households, having assured themselves of their durability.

During the next 50 years, the fused plate industry prospered. But then, as silver metal prices began to drop and labour costs increased, this labour-intensive process became progressively more expensive. After the discovery of electroplating in 1840 – a quick, inexpensive manufacturing method requiring very little silver and fewer man hours – the fused plate manufacturers were forced rapidly to adopt this new technique. To fund the new tooling required, most of the fused-plating machinery had to be scrapped. Sadly, virtually none of the original equipment exists today.

By 1850, the last fused-plate makers had either ceased to be in business or had switched to manufacturing electroplate. The industry may be dead but its legacy of often outstanding articles remains to delight future generations.

PROMINENT MAKERS

Thomas Boulsover was not an astute businessman. He freely shared his knowledge with anyone who cared to listen to him. Many did, and attempted to produce durable wares, but it was Josiah Hancock who became the first successful manufacturer of fused plate. Hancock managed to overcome most of the existing technical production problems and his skill and fine sense of style helped the industry to gain public acceptance.

The partnership formed around 1760 between Henry Tudor and Thomas Leader further advanced the industry's development. The two entrepeneurs founded a factory capable of producing large quantities of fused plate. To man it, they recruited and trained a large staff to perform specific tasks, a revolutionary concept at the time.

Another early manufacturer, Thomas Bradbury, introduced many improvements into the trade and produced articles of exceptional quality. A direct descendant, Frederick Bradbury, wrote *The History of Old Sheffield Plate,* the definitive work on the subject published in 1912. Thomas Bradbury's business survived into the 20th century under the family name, before being sold to Atkin Brothers, who in turn sold the firm's machinery and tooling to my own family in the 1960s. Bradbury's was one of the few firms to make the successful transition from Old Sheffield Plate to electroplate. Two other manufacturers worthy of note, and whose work is much sought after, were Samuel Roberts and Thomas Law. Both men worked in the mid- to late-19th century; Law was an associate of both Bradburys and Atkin Brothers.

LEFT

The letter U is the workman's stock mark, clearly visible between the manufacturer's symbols, in this case, the twin sunbursts of Matthew Boulton.

ABOVE

A stamping shop. Die-stamping allowed articles to be mass produced, and therefore more affordable.

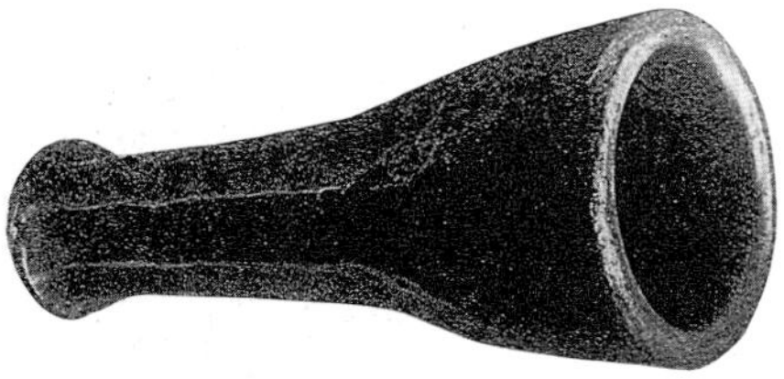

ABOVE

Drafting punch, as used in the stamping shop in the illustration above.

Unquestionably the finest exponent of Old Sheffield Plate was Matthew Boulton & Co. Volumes have been written on Matthew Boulton and his enterprise. He was an inventor and an entrepreneur, an outstanding example of the 'new industrial man'. His invaluable talent for leadership was allowed free rein by his father, a successful Birmingham toy and buckle manufacturer.

The younger Boulton, having visited Sheffield to inspect the fused plate operation, then still in its embryonic stages, set about establishing a factory in Birmingham. He installed some of the latest machinery, including some made to his own design, and employed silversmiths capable of producing excellent silverware. The double sunburst symbol, used to identify his wares, is the most desirable Old Sheffield Plate mark to be had. Consequently, his pieces command higher prices than any other maker. It is somewhat ironic that the finest Old Sheffield Plate was made in Birmingham, not Sheffield!

Besides fused plate, Boulton's factory produced sterling silverware of every kind, steel jewellery and high-quality ormolu (ground gold mixed with mercury and then gilded over brass). He worked with Robert Adam, the great architect of the late 1700s, and also Josiah Wedgwood, helping to design the interiors of some of England's greatest houses. His encouragement and financial support of James Watt led to the development of the steam engine and its many applications. Birmingham became established as the world centre for heavy machinery, contributing to Britain's pre-eminent world status at the time.

Boulton's factory was a model of ideal conditions and enlightened work practices; he was a social reformer in his home city and was greatly liked and respected by all who met him. Apart from his exceptional business acumen and skill in the silver industry, much is owed to him for his diverse contributions outside his own field. Examples of his work can be seen in museums throughout Britain and the United States, as well as in English stately homes.

Other makers of prominence were T & J Creswick; James Dixon & Sons; Roberts, Smith & Co, J Watson & Son; Waterhouse, Hatfield & Co, and H Wilkinson & Co. These were all 19th-century firms who produced high-standard goods in prolific quantities.

THE PROCESS

Coating silver over steel, iron, copper, brass and various other base metals had been tried with unsatisfactory results prior to the 1740s. These early attempts were often perpetrated by silversmiths wishing to deceive the public by selling objects resembling sterling silver – thankfully with little success. Acts of Parliament were passed from the reign of Henry IV onwards, to prohibit the practice. However, it was legal to burnish beaten leaves of silver onto base metal. As such a low heat was used, the metals rarely adhered properly and the effect was cheap and tinsely. The method, only used for small items such as knives and spurs, lasted into the 19th century.

Most of the early experimentation involved covering steel with silver, refered to as close-plating. The major drawback was steel's tendency to rust under the silver, causing the surface to bubble and the eventual disintegration of the whole object. The accidental discovery that copper and silver could be married together to good effect did not have an immediate impact on the silver trade. It took almost 20 years for the process to be developed fully to become Old

A copper ingot was covered by one or more sheets of sterling silver. All touching surfaces had to be scrupulously clean. A copper sheet, whitewashed on its inner surface, was then wrapped around the silver-covered ingot. This in turn was tied with iron wire and then borax paste applied to the exposed junction between the copper ingot and silver cover to act as a flux. Without this flux, the two metals would oxidize and fusion would not occur.

The whole block was then heated in a furnace and removed once the metals began to melt. The wires were cut and the outer copper sheet removed, leaving the silver sheets fused to the copper ingot where their surfaces met. Finally, the block was cooled and put through rollers to reduce it to sheet form. The sheet, viewed sideways on, resembled a metal sandwich; two thin layers of sterling silver separated in the middle by a thicker copper filling. From this fused sheet, the silversmith could fashion his wares.

IDENTIFYING OLD SHEFFIELD PLATE

As there was no continuous system agreed by manufacturers for marking Old Sheffield Plate products, style and construction methods are the only correct means of identifying items and dating them.

ABOVE

Copper ingot covered in a sheet of sterling silver, prior to the fusing process.

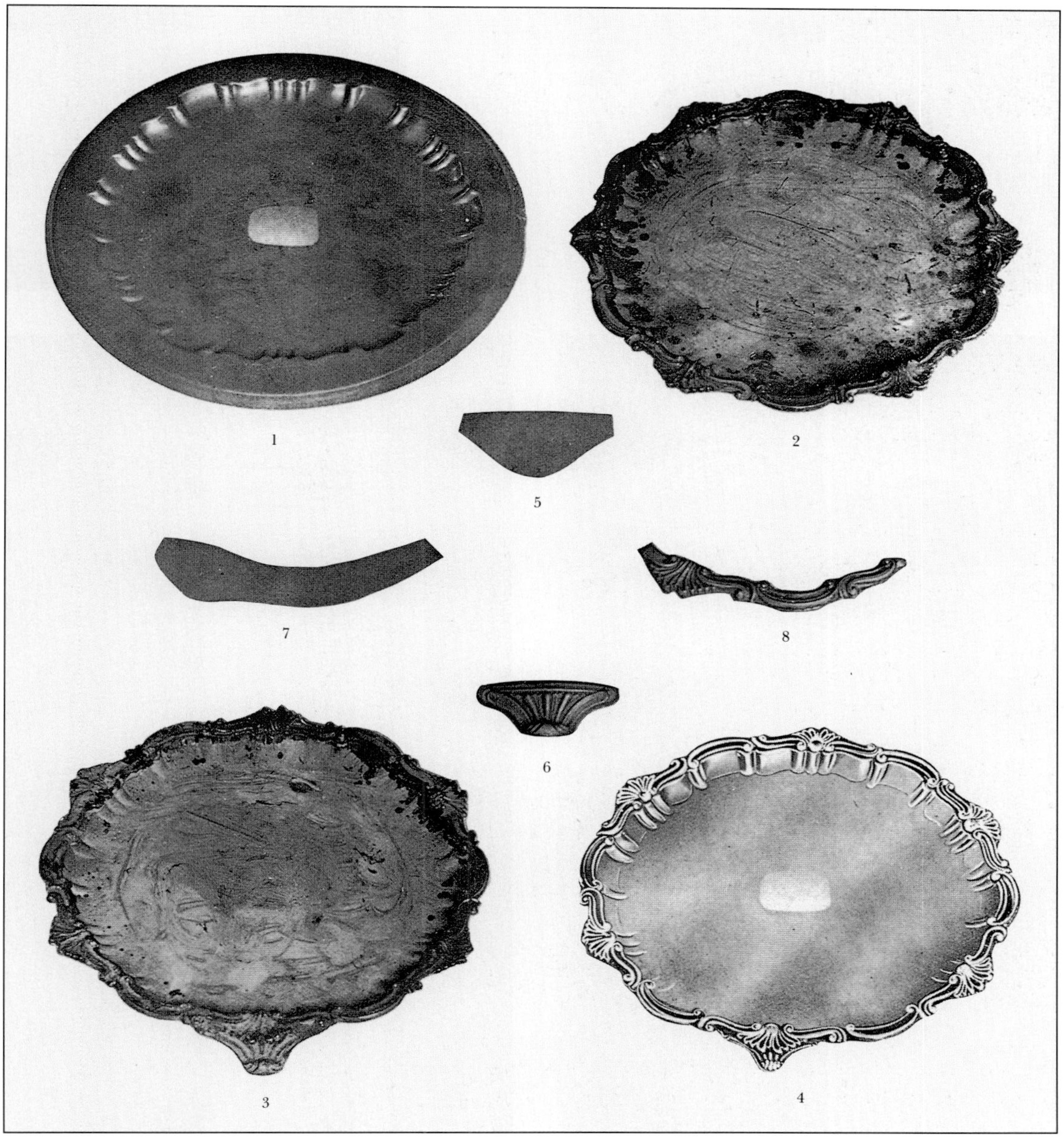

RIGHT

Stages of making a fused plate salver: 1) The salver is blank stamped from fused plate. 2) The mounts are soldered on. 3) The feet are soldered on. 4) The completed salver. 5) The foot cut out of silver prior to stamping. 6) The foot, stamped, and filled with lead tin, before being soldered onto the salver. 7) The unstamped mount. 8) The stamped, filled mount, before soldering.

LEFT

Drawn wire work forming the gallery border of a bottle coaster *c.* 1780. The drawn wire technique was both complicated and costly because thick copper wire had to be coated in sterling silver and drawn through rollers in order to obtain a thin fine wire.

LEFT

Here, drawn wire has been used and a machine punched open work gallery is surmounted by gadroon pattern applied borders. Coaster *c.* 1795.

ABOVE

Hand-pierced decoration on a mustard pot *c.* 1780.

TOP RIGHT

Punched decoration (underside view) of a candlestick nozzle, also showing the rolled under edge *c.* 1770.

LEFT

The top side and underside of a salver. Notice the hand-chasing is visible on the back as well as the front. Also visible on the underside is the rolled edge of the applied border and a faint showing of copper where the rolled edge has been lost.

To confirm that a piece is Old Sheffield Plate, it should be examined for evidence of the following manufacturers' techniques:

- rolled edges
- grey-coloured solder on mounts and borders
- visible copper base metal (bleeding)
- seams
- tinned undersides and interiors
- applied, let-in or rubbed-in shields

Because styles changed about every 10 years, it is possible to establish an approximate date for fused plate pieces. As it was very rare for makers to repeat previous designs, dating is not very difficult. A representative sample is included in this chapter. For a more in-depth look at styles, see Chapter 5.

ABOVE AND LEFT

An applied border with rolled edge as seen from the top and underneath.

BELOW

Silver mounts or borders (top and bottom view) before they are cut and filled with lead and affixed to the article.

ROLLED EDGES

During the mid 1840s to 1850s, one also can find articles that were produced using many of the Old Sheffield Plate methods except that they did not fuse the sterling silver to the copper but instead used copper sheet metal and peripheral silver mounts and stampings, all of which were then electroplated. Articles produced using this combination of two methods are referred to as coming from the 'transitional' period. Because the sheet metal had edges exposing the copper core, it was necessary, when formed to cover them up to make silverware usable and attractive. Prior to 1775, patterns such as beading were punched into rims and edges with the exposed copper pressed underneath. This can be particularly observed on coffee pot lids and bases, as well as on candlestick nozzles.

From 1775 onwards, a popular method of concealing the raw edge was to apply borders of silver wire or thin fused plate wire. Later pieces have thin silver mounts, usually decorated in a fashionable pattern of the period, applied to the rim, with the edge folded over to cover the copper. During the last period of manufacture in the 1840s, a more cost-effective technique for finishing was developed. This involved bevelling the edge, thus creating a smooth finish which exposed the metal layers on the underside.

The rolled edge is one of the best ways of telling that a piece is Old Sheffield Plate; scrape your nail against the underside edge of a piece to feel this rolled finish.

SOLDER-ON MOUNTS AND BORDERS

As described, applied borders were usually of thin silver. These hollow stampings had little strength to withstand the wear and tear of daily use. To give additional support, mounts were filled with lead-based soft solder. Where a thin silver mount has worn through, the solder is visible; excessive exposure is a sign of considerable use. This wear is detrimental to the appearance of the item and its value. Many of the supports and handles on Old Sheffield Plate were also thin decorative stampings, filled with the same soft solder and then applied to the main body.

It should be noted that some of the earliest pieces were made with brass as the base metal, though it soon became apparent that its adhesive properties were not as good as copper and its use was discontinued. A few examples survive.

FAR LEFT

The 'key' seam, a similar principle to a dovetail join in furniture, was considered a stronger join than the straight seam and therefore denoted better quality.

LEFT AND BELOW

A let-in shield as it is seen on the outside of a coffee pot, and the view from the inside. The let-in shield has been engraved, which otherwise would not have been possible on the surface of this Old Sheffield article as doing so would expose the copper beneath. The shield is not always visible on the inside as it is here. Different methods for putting in the shield sometimes provide a near perfect hidden base on which to engrave.

OPPOSITE

Parts of die-stamped candlesticks, prior to construction.

VISIBLE COPPER BASE METAL (BLEEDING)

For identification purposes, never assume that copper (or brass) showing through on articles automatically indicates Old Sheffield Plate, without other corrobating evidence. Copper is often used in electroplate production.

SEAMS

As all Old Sheffield hollow ware was made from sheet metal, a joining seam is nearly always visible. When locating the seam, look inside the object first, then outside. If it's still not in evidence, try breathing on the piece, which should reveal even the best-hidden join.

TINNED UNDERSIDES AND INTERIORS

It is important to remember that Old Sheffield Plate was considered a 'poor man's silver', its main purpose being to provide attractive, functional articles that looked just like sterling silver. Indeed, the surface of these objects *was* sterling silver, and the whole was available at a fraction of the cost of the solid version. A cost-cutting exercise developed around the late 1700s which used tin on unseen surfaces instead of sterling silver – particularly on the undersides of trays, salvers and urn bases, or inside articles such as teapots, coffee pots, meat dish covers and entrée dish warmers. No guest would be rude enough to examine the underside of your serving tray, or servant divulge the secret of the teapot! The tinning process was simply accomplished by substituting a layer of tin for the silver on one side of the ingot before fusing. The sandwich of sheet metal would thus consist of sterling silver and tin with a copper centre. Tinning was only used for the Old Sheffield Plate process, so its presence is an indication that the piece is not electroplated.

APPLIED, LET-IN OR RUBBED-IN SHIELDS

When the British aristocracy finally decided to buy Old Sheffield Plate, it was necessary to provide a specific plate on objects where family crests could be engraved. Engraving directly onto the fused plate surface would cut through the sterling silver, exposing the copper base metal beneath. To overcome this problem a fused plate shield with an extra-thick silver covering – or, at more expense, a solid sterling silver shield – was soldered into place. Later this technique was modified and the shield was 'let-in', that is to say, a hole was cut into the article allowing the shield to be soldered into it, flush with the surface, and to look like an integral part of it. The surface would be burnished to disguise the join. This method became more sophisticated *c.* 1810, when a thin, fine pure silver disc was rubbed into the surface by burnishing.

Inserts accomplished by the last two methods can usually be seen with the naked eye on the centre of salvers and trays or the sides of hollow ware articles. Once again, try breathing on the area to show up the insertion.

Another method for adding engraved work, especially bright cut engraving, was to apply ready-worked sterling or fine silver bands which sat proud on the body of the article. This form of adornment was prevalent during the latter part of the 18th century.

Other techniques were employed in the embellishment of fused silver which were not unique to the manufacture of Old Sheffield Plate. Drawn wire was used to make openwork baskets and decanter coasters, although producing it was difficult and costly. Thick copper wire was wrapped in sterling silver, then drawn through rollers to obtain a thin, fine wire. This practice started as early as 1765 and continued through most of the fused plate production period. Pierced decoration, either cut by hand, or later punched by machine, was also popular during the 1790s.

By the early 1800s, tastes inclined towards more elaborate forms of decoration. It was during this period that chasing –

and also flat-chasing – on Old Sheffield Plate were perfected. Usually the fused metal sheet was flat-chased by being laid onto a bed of pitch or tar, then decorations would be punched into the metal using chasing tools. The backing of soft pitch allowed the alloy metal to give without piercing. The sheet, once chased, would then be formed into its destined use. Check the underside or inside of silverware to identify chasing/flat-chasing, as the decoration will be visible on both sides because of the punched or hammered nature of the process.

Die-stamping was used in mass production, allowing candlesticks, etc, to be produced at affordable prices. This cost-cutting technique was also used to stamp out mounts, spouts and other additions.

Sometimes hallmarked sterling silver parts were added to Old Sheffield Plate. These included detachable handles for entrée dishes or finials for tea and coffee pots. For this reason do not assume that an article is sterling silver just because there is a hallmark on a detachable part of it. Given that the attached part is contemporary with the whole, the hallmark will give the year of manufacture.

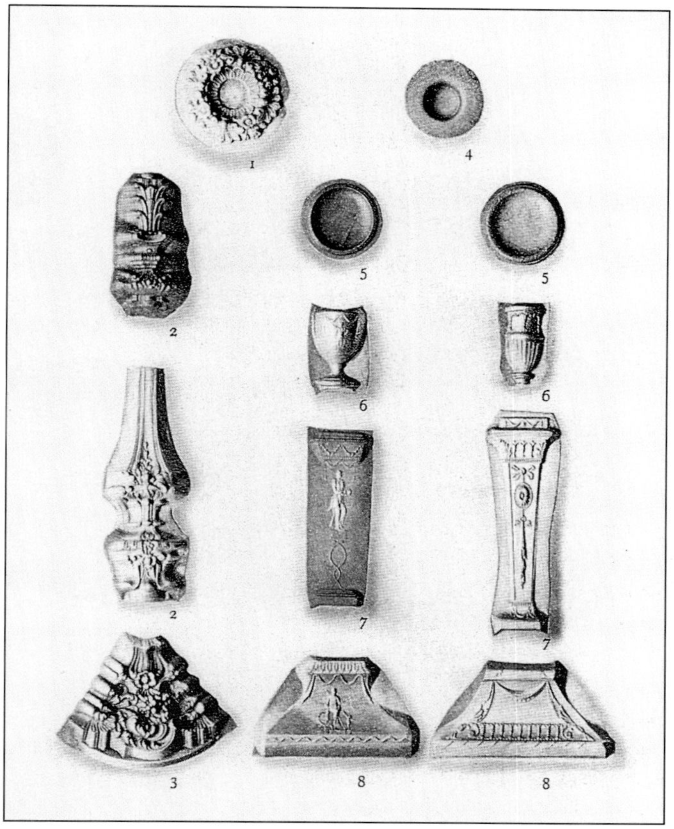

LEGISLATION AND MARKINGS

There are no hallmarks on Old Sheffield Plate simply because there was no legal obligation to do so. In fact, gold and silversmiths lobbied vigorously to prevent fused plate hallmarks. As the inclusion of makers' symbols and names was not compulsory, only about 25 per cent of Old Sheffield Plate has any makers' marks at all.

Many early marks were stamped to mislead the public into thinking that the articles were, in fact, hallmarked sterling silver. This practice was eliminated during the late 1700s, following the establishment of the Sheffield and Birmingham assay offices. Legislation was created to prevent fused plate makers imitating hallmarks, with the introduction of large fines and imprisonment to deter possible offenders.

Other than the few registered makers' marks and symbols, only initials or numbers next to stamped London retailers' names exist. These were probably stock accounting marks to help with reordering, as much of the output from Sheffield and Birmingham was sold to the cream of British and world outlets. When identifying Old Sheffield Plate, a maker's mark is a great bonus.

ADVANTAGES AND DISADVANTAGES OF FUSED PLATE IN USE

Fused plate, with its durable covering of sterling silver, was perfectly functional for daily use at the time of manufacture. Some items, now over 200 years old, still have their original coating. The sterling silver fused with its base metal was far stronger than an electroplate surface, the soft, pure silver coating of which wears through relatively quickly. But old pieces with original coatings are likely to show exposed copper on parts that have been polished vigorously. This is known as bleeding.

The main weakness of Old Sheffield Plate is the solder points, where handles and spouts are joined to the main body. Soft solder was the joining material, which is prone to break away completely or cause leakage around the spouts.

Only the best silversmiths nowadays are capable of restoring Old Sheffield Plate and the cost can be expensive. Do request a quotation for repairs before purchasing Old Sheffield Plate in need of restoration. An article that has been painstakingly restored to a good standard of condition has years of use ahead and is a pleasure to own.

REPLATING

Replating any Old Sheffield Plate should be seen as a last resort measure. Electroplating is the only option available, but it will give pieces an unflattering shiny bright new appearance, changing the colour from the original soft blue lustre of aged sterling silver to the white glare of pure silver.

The best guideline is only to replate articles that have more than 70 per cent copper bleeding through. By the time this amount of copper is exposed, approximately 50 per cent of the item's value has been lost. Replating in these circumstances will give another lease of life without further diminishing the value.

Good silversmiths can replate and give an 'antique' finish to dull down the bright lustre of electroplating. This is achieved by a combination of scratch brushing the new surface and oxidizing. Do seek expert advice before replating.

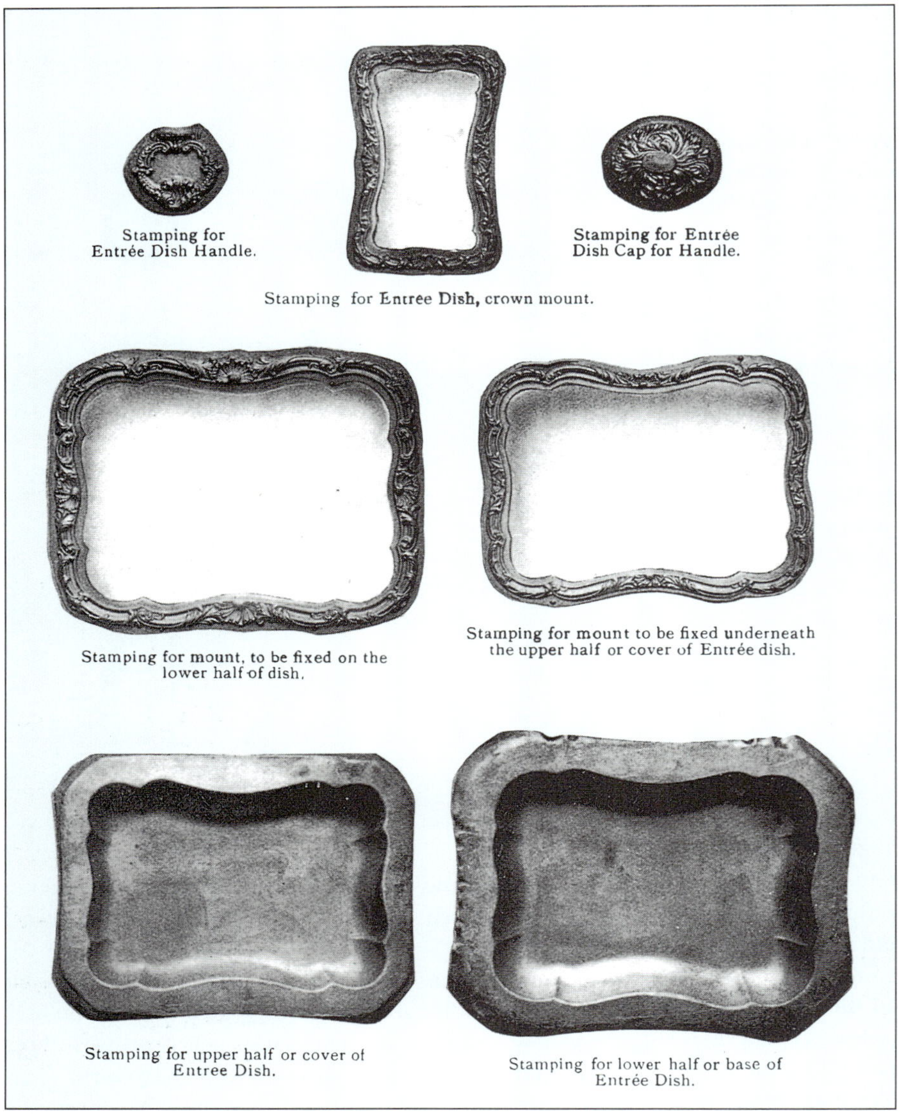

ABOVE

Die-stamped pieces for the construction of an entrée dish.

LEFT

An Old Sheffield fruit basket with swing handle *c.* 1830. The construction methods employed were never completely satisfactory for producing a strong usable handle and breaks often occur in this area. Here is a typical repair, the lead solder clearly visible.

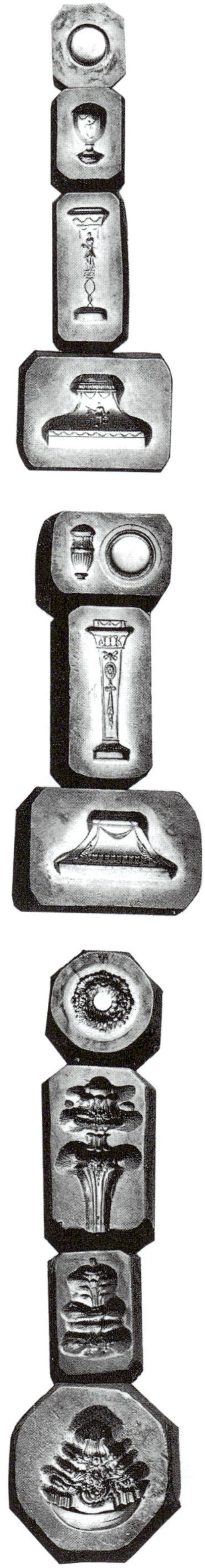

RIGHT

Dies for stamping candlesticks.

OLD SHEFFIELD PLATE MARKS

NAME OF FIRM	MAKER'S MARK	DATE
Fox T. & Co	FOX.PROCTOR PASMORE & Co	1784
Green W. & Co.	W.GREEN &Co	1784
Holy D., Wilkinson & Co.	DAN HOLY WILKINSON & Co	1784
Law T. & Co.	THOs LAW & Co	1784
Parsons J. & Co.	JOHN PARSONS & Co	1784
Smith N. & Co.	N·SMITH & Co	1784
Staniforth, Parkin & Co.	STANIFORTH PARKIN&Co	1784
Sykes & Co.	SYKES &Co	1784
Tudor, Leader & Nicholson	TUDOR&Co	1784
Boulton M. & Co.	BOULTON	1784
Dixon T. & Co.	DIXON &Co	1784
Holland H. & Co.	HOLLAND&Co	1784
Moore J.	Moore MOORE §	1784
Smith & Co.	SMITH&Co	1784
Beldon, Hoyland & Co.	BELDON HOYLAND &Co	1785
Brittain, Wilkinson & Brownill	BRITTAIN WILKIN SON & BROWNILL	1785
Deakin, Smith & Co.	DEAKIN SMITH &Co	1785
Love J. & Co. (Love, Silverside, Darby & Co)	I.LOVE&Co	1785
Morton R. & Co.	MORTON&Co	1785
Roberts, Cadman & Co.		1785
Roberts J. & S.	I&S ROBERTS	1786
Sutcliffe R. & Co.		1786
Bingley W.	W.BINGLEY	1787
Madin F. & Co.	F.MADIN&Co	1788

NAME OF FIRM	MAKER'S MARK	DATE
Colmore S.	S C Colmore Patent	1790
Goodwin E.	E GOODWIN	1794
Watson, Fenton & Bradbury	WATSON&Co	1795
Froggatt, Coldwell & Lean	FROGGATT COLDWELL & LEAN	1797
Green J. & Co.	I·GREEN&Co	1799
Goodman, Gainsford & Fairbairn	A·GOODMAN&Co	1800
Ellerby W.	ELL ER BY	1803
Garnett W.	GARNETT	1803
Holy D., Parker & Co.	DAN HOLY PARKER & Co	1804
Newbould W. & Son	W. NEWBOULD & SON	1804
Drabble I. & Co.	I.DRABBLE &Co	1805
Coldwell W.	W.COLDWELL.	1806
Hill D. & Co.	HILL HILL&Co	1806
Law J. & Son	LAW & SON	1807
Butts T.	TB S	1807
Green J.	GREEN	1807
Hutton W.	Hutton	1807
Law R.	R.LAW.	1807
Linwood J.	I·LIN WOOD	1807
Linwood W.	LIN WOOD	1807
Meredith H.	MERE DITH	1807
Peake	PEAKE	1807
Ryland W. & Son	RYLAND	1807
Scot W.		1807
Silkirk W.	Sil-kirk	1807

NAME OF FIRM	MAKER'S MARK	DATE
Thomason E. & Dowler	THOMASON	1807
Tonks Samuel	TONKS	1807
Waterhouse & Co.	WATERHOUSE&Co	1807
Wilmore Joseph	PATENT WILLMORE & WILKES	1807
Gainsford R	GAINSFORD GA	1808
Hatfield A.	A H	1808
Banister W.	BANI STER	1808
Gibbs G.		1808
Hipkiss J.	HIPKISS	1808
Horton D.	D·HORTON	1808
Lea A. C.	A·C·LEA	1808
Linwood M. & Sons	LIN WOOD	1808
Nichols J.	J·NICHOLDS	1808
Beldon G.	BEL DON	1809
Wright J. & Fairbairn G.	WRIGHT FAIRBAIRN	1809
Cheston T.	Ches ton	1809
Harrison J.	HARRI SON	1809
Hipwood W.	HIP WOOD	1809
Horton J.	HOR TON	1809
Silk R.		1809
Howard S. & T.	How ard	1809
Smith, Tate, Nicholson & Hoult		1810
Dunn G. B.	DUNN	1810
Hanson M.	HAN SON	1810
Pimley S.		1810
Creswick T. & J.		1811
Stot B.	Stot	1811
Watson, Pass & Co. (late J. Watson)	WATSON PASS & Co	1811
Lees G.	LEES	1811
Pearson R.	PEAR SON	1811
White J. (White & Allgood)	WHITE	1811
Kirkby S.	KIRKBY FOR·USE	1812
Allgood J.	ALL GOOD	1812
Allport E.	All port	1812
Gilbert J.		1812
Hinks J.	HINKS	1812
Johnson J.	JOHN SON	1812
Small T.	SMALL	1812
Smith W.	SM ITH	1812
Younge S. & C. & Co.	S.C.YOUNGE &Co	1813
Thomas S.	THO MAS	1813
Tyndall J.	TYN DALL	1813
Best H.		1814
Cracknall J.	CRACK NALL	1814
Jordan T.	JOR DAN	1814
Woodward W.		1814
Lilly, John	LILLY	1815
Best & Wastidge	BEST	1816
Ashley	ASH LEY	1816
Davis J.	DAVIS	1816
Evans S.	S·EVANS	1816
Freeth H	FREETH HF	1816

NAME OF FIRM	MAKER'S MARK	DATE
Harwood T.		1816
Lilly, Joseph		1816
Turley S.		1816
Cope C. G.		1817
Pemberton & Mitchell		1817
Shephard J.		1817
Markland W.		1818
Corn J. & J. Sheppard		1819
Rogers J.		1819
Hall W.		1820
Moore F.		1820
Turton J.		1820
Blagden, Hodgson & Co.		1821
Holy D. & G.		1821
Needham C.		1821
Sansom T. & Sons		1821
Child T.		1821
Smith I.		1821
Worton S.		1821
Rodgers J. & Sons		1822
Bradshaw J.		1822
Briggs W.		1823
Harrison G.		1823
Smallwood J.		1823
Causer J. F.		1824
Jones		1824
Tonks & Co.		1824
Robarts, Smith & Co.		1828
Smith J. & Son		1828
Askew		1828
Hall, Henry		1829
Hobday J.		1829
Watson J. and Son		1830
Bishop, Thomas		1830
Hutton W.		1831
Atkin, Henry		1833
Waterhouse I. & I. & Co.		1833
Watson W.		1833
Dixon J. & Sons		1835
Smith J.		1836
Waterhouse, Hatfield & Co.		1836
Wilkinson H. & Co.		1836
Hutton W.		1837
Hutton W.		1839

NAME OF FIRM	MAKER'S MARK	DATE
Prime J.		1839
Walker, Knowles & Co.		1840
Waterhouse, George & Co.		1842
Smith, Sissons & Co.		1848
Padley, Parkin & Co.		1849
Hutton W.		1849
Mappin Bros.		1850
Oldham T.		1860
Roberts & Briggs		1860

OPPOSITE
William IV covered dish. Although the dish itself is made of sterling silver, the base and hot water jacket are made of Old Sheffield Plate.

MISCELLANEOUS MARKS

MAKER'S MARKS	APPROXIMATE DATE
	1780–1790
	1790
	1790
	1790–1800
Do.	1790–1800
	1800–1810
	1815–1825
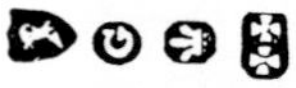	1815–1825
	1815–1825
GILBERT LONDON	1840
	1840
	1840
	1840
	1850
	1850
	1850
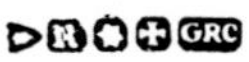	1850

ELECTROPLATE MARKS

The following are registered trademarks, mainly found on electroplate, although many of the companies also produced sterling silver articles.

ALLEN & MARTIN
BIRMINGHAM

ALUMINIUM CO LTD
LONDON

H A

ARCHER & COMPANY
SHEFFIELD

HA

ARCHER, MACHIN & MARSH
SHEFFIELD

TRADE MARK

ARMSTRONG, STEVENS & SON
BIRMINGHAM

ARMY & NAVY CO-OP SOCIETY LTD
WESTMINSTER

BRITANNIA

ASHBERRY, PHILIP & SONS
SHEFFIELD

A&S

ASTON, T & SON
BIRMINGHAM

H.A HA FA FA A B S

ATKIN BROTHERS TRURO
SHEFFIELD

H.A

ATKIN, HENRY
SHEFFIELD

BRILHO

ATKINSON BROTHERS
MILTON WORKS, SHEFFIELD

TB&C

BADGER, T
SHEFFIELD

BW&A

BADGER, WORRALL & ARMITAGE
SHEFFIELD

MERIT

BAKER, JOHN & COMPANY
WHEELDON WORKS, SHEFFIELD

ORIEL NICKEL SILVER

BARKER BROTHERS
BIRMINGHAM

BARNASCONE, LEWIS
SHEFFIELD

DURATION RECTO DURATION

BARNES, FREDERICK & CO
LONDON, BIRMINGHAM & SHEFFIELD

FUSI YAMA SPHINX BRAND

BATT, JOHN & COMPANY
LONDON

W B & S

BATT, WILLIAM & SONS
SHEFFIELD

SILVERINE IS EQUAL TO STERLING SILVER IN WEAR & APPEARANCE SILVERINE

BAUM, MAURICE
SHEFFIELD

BEACH & MINTE

BEACH & MINTE
BIRMINGHAM

BEAL, J & J
REDHILL WORKS, SHEFFIELD

MB

BEAL, M
SHEFFIELD

AB & Co AB

BEARDSHAW, A J & CO
SHEFFIELD

J&JB

BELL, J & J
SHEFFIELD

IB

BELL, JOHN
SHEFFIELD

BELL, JONATHAN
SHEFFIELD

J.W. Benson

BENSON, J W
LONDON

JB JB

BIGGIN, JOHN
SHEFFIELD

BINGHAM & OGDEN
SHEFFIELD

BW & Co
WARRANTED
SILVER SOLDERED.

BINGLEY, GEORGE BOWER
SHEFFIELD

THE SHROPSHIRE AND NORTH WALES
GENERAL SUPPLY STORES
33 PRIDE HILL, SHREWSBURY.
R. BINNALL & CO. PROPRIETORS.

BINNALL, R & CO
SHREWSBURY

BIRTS & SONS HIRE PURCHASE SYSTEM
WITHIN
THE REACH OF
ALL.

BIRTS & SON
WOOLWICH

BISHOP, GEORGE & SONS
SHEFFIELD

GENIUS.

BLYDE, JOHN
CLINTOCK WORKS, SHEFFIELD

CB

BOARDMAN, C
SHEFFIELD

BOARDMAN, GLOSSOP & CO
CLARENCE WORKS, SHEFFIELD

BOLSOVER, HENRY
PORTLAND WORKS, SHEFFIELD

WE LIVE IN STIRRING TIMES.

BONSER & SON
LONDON

SILVERSTEIN.

BOX, W R & COMPANY
DUBLIN

TB&S

BRADBURY, THOMAS & SONS
SHEFFIELD

TOPAZ.

BRADLEY, ALBERT SAMUEL
SHEFFIELD

EB

BRADLEY, E
SHEFFIELD

RELIABLE
THE MASHER

BRAMWELL, BROWNHILL & CO
SHEFFIELD

WB

BREARLEY, W
SHEFFIELD

B.B
AB FB

BRIDDON BROTHERS
VICTORIA PLATE WORKS, SHEFFIELD

S B & Co

BRIGHT, S & COMPANY
SHEFFIELD

BRITTAIN, S & COMPANY
ST GEORGE'S WORKS, SHEFFIELD

B&C

BROOKES & CROOKES
ATLANTIC WORKS, SHEFFIELD

HELMET BRAND

BROOKS, HENRY & CO
LONDON

BROWETT, ALFRED
BIRMINGHAM

BRITISH

BROWETT, ASHBERRY & CO
BIRMINGHAM

B&C

BROWN & CLARK
BIRMINGHAM

B C C

CHANTRILL & COMPANY
BIRMINGHAM

HESSIN.

CHARLES, ANDREW
BIRMINGHAM

LAUS VARIETAS

CHARLTON BROTHERS
BIRMINGHAM

J C & Co

CHESTERMAN, JAMES & CO
BOW WORKS, SHEFFIELD

C C
CHRISTOFLE

CHRISTOFLE & COMPANY
PARIS

CLARKS
JUBILEE GOLD

CLARK, JOHN
BIRMINGHAM

MONTANA SILVER.
Collings & Wallis

COLLINGS & WALLIS
BIRMINGHAM

COLLINS, CHARLES HOWARD
BIRMINGHAM

CO-OP WHOLESALE SOCIETY, LTD
MANCHESTER

XX

COPLEY, JOHN & SONS
RICHMOND WORKS, SHEFFIELD

J.Y.C

COWLISHAW, J Y
SHEFFIELD

ARCAS

COWPER-COLES, COWPER BICKERTON
LONDON

CRESWICK & Co.

C&Co

CRESWICK & COMPANY
SHEFFIELD

CRESWICK, T J & N
SHEFFIELD

BLUE RIBBON ARMY

CULF, ARTHUR
SHEFFIELD

I.P.C

CUTTS, J P
SHEFFIELD

RAENO

DAFFERN, WILLIAM
BIRMINGHAM

TRADE MARK

INDIAN SILVER

NEVADA SILVER

ALUMINIUM SILVER

BRAZILIAN SILVER

BENGAL SILVER

JAPANESE SILVER

LAXEY SILVER

ARGENLINE

BURMAROID

DANIEL & ARTER
GLOBE NEVADA SILVER WORKS, BIRMINGHAM

GD

DEAKIN, G & COMPANY
SHEFFIELD

DEAKIN, JAMES & SONS
SHEFFIELD

PLENTY

PHOENIX WORKS

DERBY, JOHN & SONS
SHEFFIELD

"STANDARD" ELECTRO PLATE SPOONS, FORKS, &c.

"ROYAL STANDARD"

"ROYAL STANDARD" VICTORIA SILVER

"STANDARD" VICTORIA SILVER

DERRY, FREDERICK
BIRMINGHAM

JD&S

DIXON

DIXON, JAMES & SONS
SHEFFIELD

W&MD WD

DODGE, W & M
MANCHESTER

GUANACO

DOUGHTY, ALEXANDER & CO
LIVERPOOL

GUANACO

DRYSDALE, J & J & CO
LONDON

DYSON, JOHN
LEEDS

TE

EATON, T W
SHEFFIELD

CE

EDWARDS, GEORGE
GLASGOW

EGLENTINE

EGLINGTON, F
STAFFORDSHIRE

E&Co

ELKINGTON

ELKINGTON & Co

ELKINGTON

ELKINGTON & Co

ELKINGTON

ELKINGTON & CO, LTD
BIRMINGHAM

E M & Co

ELKINGTON, MASON & CO
BIRMINGHAM

C E & Co

ELLIS, CHARLES & CO
SHEFFIELD

PRIMUS ISAAC ELLIS & SONS. SHEFFIELD.

ELLIS, ISAAC & SONS
SHEFFIELD

T.E

ELLIS, T
PLYMOUTH

ELMORE, JOHN S & CO
LONDON

SAVARS.

EVANS, LESCHER & WEBB
LONDON

SAVARS.

EVANS SONS & CO
LIVERPOOL

FARROW & JACKSON

LONDON & PARIS.

FARROW & JACKSON
LONDON

THE GOLDEN CUPID

Wedding and Keeper Ring

ESTABLISHMENT

FEAR, EDWIN
BRISTOL

F&A

FENTON & ANDERTON
SHEFFIELD

FBR JFF &FF

FENTON BROTHERS
SHEFFIELD

J·F·F

FENTON, J F
SHEFFIELD

JF

FENTON, JAMES
BIRMINGHAM

G B

FIELD, ALFRED & CO
BIRMINGHAM & SHEFFIELD

SILVENE

FIELDING, HENRY
BIRMINGHAM

TF

FREEMAN, T
SHEFFIELD

W.G WG

GALLIMORE, W & CO
SHEFFIELD

GLACIARIUM CARAFE

GANGEE, JOHN
THE GLACIARIUM, MIDDLESEX

1376

GARFITT, THOMAS & SON
CROSS SCYTHES WORKS, SHEFFIELD

J C ALMADA SILVER ARGENTINA SILVER *Joseph Gilbert* JG

GILBERT, JOSEPH
SUN WORKS, BIRMINGHAM

G&S LTD

GILBERT & SPURRIER, LTD
BIRMINGHAM

ARGOSY SILVER

GILDING & SILVERING CO
MIDDLESEX

"PATRIOT"

GLAUERT, L & C
SHEFFIELD

GOLDSMITHS' ALLIANCE, LTD
LONDON

BB

GOODALL, HENRY ARTHUR
LONDON

GOODE, JOHN & SONS
BIRMINGHAM

ARGOSY SILVER

GORER, SOLOMON LEWIS
MIDDLESEX

TRADE MARK G&C TORO G C B G.C. B.

GOTSCHER & COMPANY
BIRMINGHAM

BRITISH

GRAYSON, BENJAMIN
SHEFFIELD

G&C

GREEN, J
SHEFFIELD

GRINSELL & SONS
LONDON

TIP

HALE BROTHERS
SHEFFIELD

MAZEPPA

HANCOCK, SAMUEL & SONS
MAZEPPA WORKS, SHEFFIELD

HANDS, THOMAS
BIRMINGHAM

PERUVIAN SILVER

HANDS & SONS
BIRMINGHAM

V R HARRISON BROS & HOWSON CUTLERS TO HER MAJESTY ALPHA HH

HARRISON BROTHERS & HOWSON
SHEFFIELD

I·H

HARRISON, J & CO
NORFOLK WORKS, SHEFFIELD

HARRISON, J
SHEFFIELD

W W H WWH WWH

HARRISON, W W & CO
MONTGOMERY WORKS, SHEFFIELD

GH

HAWKSLEY, G
SHEFFIELD

GH&Co GH CH

HAWKSLEY, G & CO
SHEFFIELD

CH JE JKB TH GW PERFECTION PERFECTION Siberian Silver SIBERIAN SILVER

HAWKSWORTH, EYRE & CO
SHEFFIELD

SOLE PROPRIETORS
PERFECTION
SOLE PROPRIETORS

HAYMAN & COMPANY
BIRMINGHAM

HECKFORD, ARTHUR EGERTON
BIRMINGHAM

AFRICAN SILVER

HILLS, MENKE & CO
BIRMINGHAM

XPRESS

HOBSON, HENRY & SONS
LONDON & SHEFFIELD

R. HODD & SON LONDON

HODD, A & SONS
MIDDLESEX

HOPE, J V & HOPE G F W
ATLANTIC WORKS, WEDNESBURY & LONDON

WELL DONE

HOWARD, FRANCIS
ABERDEEN WORKS, SHEFFIELD

HOWARTH, JAMES & SONS
SHEFFIELD

The "Sceptre"
"Jubilee"

HOWELL & JAMES, LTD
LONDON

H&F

HUKIN & FENTON
BIRMINGHAM

HUKIN & HEATH
BIRMINGHAM

RADIANT

HUMPHREYS, W R & CO
SHEFFIELD

LLAMA
FUERTE

HUNTER, MICHAEL & SON
TALBOT WORKS, SHEFFIELD

HUTTON, WILLIAM & SONS
SHEFFIELD & LONDON

IBBERSON, GEORGE
SHEFFIELD

BALMAIN

IHLEE & HORNE
LONDON

SILVERODE

INGRAM, JOHN
BIRMINGHAM

JACKSON, WILLIAM & CO
SHEAF ISLAND WORKS, SHEFFIELD

LEVIATHAN.

JAMES, JOHN & SONS
VICTORIA WORKS, REDDITCH

RMJ & CO

JOHNSON, R M & CO
SHOREHAM PLATE WORKS, SHEFFIELD

PILOT

JONES, C
LIVERPOOL

THE CYPRUS

JUDD & COMPANY
LONDON

STERLING BRAND

KEEP BROTHERS
BIRMINGHAM

KNIGHT, HENRY & CO
LONDON

IK &S

KNOWLES, J & SON
SHEFFIELD

KOERBER & COMPANY
LONDON

GLORIOUS.

LANDER, EDWIN & CO
BIRMINGHAM

LEE, WILLIAM & SONS
SHEFFIELD

L&M

LEE & MIDDLETON
SHEFFIELD

ALBION SILVER

LEE & WIGFULL
JOHN STREET WORKS, SHEFFIELD

SUNLIGHT

LEVER BROTHERS
PORT SUNLIGHT

LB LB

LEVESLEY BROTHERS
CENTRAL WORKS, SHEFFIELD

TRADE MARK KINGTONS METAL
CANADIAN GOLD
L.B.CANADA
TRADE MARK SIBERIAN GOLD A PERFECT IMITATION OF FINE GOLD.
"KARANTI SILVER"
GOLDTECTA
"ECLIPSE SOVEREIGN PURSE

LEVETUS BROTHERS
BIRMINGHAM

LEVY BROTHERS
LONDON

LEVY, M de J & SONS
LONDON

LLOYD, TAYLOR & CO
LONDON

MONKEY

C X

LB

LOCKWOOD BROTHERS, LTD
SHEFFIELD

LONG, HAWKSLEY & CO
HALLAMSHIRE WORKS, SHEFFIELD

TPL

LOWE, T P
SHEFFIELD

M&C

MACKAY & CHISHOLM
EDINBURGH

BRENADA SILVER
J. R. McC.

McCLELLAND, JAMES ROBERT
SHEFFIELD

McDONALD & COMPANY
BIRMINGHAM & WHITBY

M T R

McEWAN, JAMES & CO, LTD
LONDON

M B R

McLEAN BROTHERS & RIGG, LTD
LONDON

NICKELINE

McMURTRIE, JOHN McLEOWNAN
GLASGOW

MAIGATTER, CARL
LONDON

E J M

MAKIN, E J
SHEFFIELD

M B Co

MAMMATT, BUXTON & CO
ARUNDEL PLATE WORKS, SHEFFIELD

MANTON, J S & CO
BIRMINGHAM

MB MB EM JM EM JM

MAPPIN BROS

MAPPIN BROTHERS
QUEENS WORKS, SHEFFIELD & LONDON

J N M Co

MAPPIN & COMPANY
ROYAL CUTLERY WORKS, SHEFFIELD

M&B

MAPPIN, JOSEPH & BROTHERS
SHEFFIELD

J.M

MAPPIN & SON
SHEFFIELD

MW&Co

MAPPIN, WEBB & CO
SHEFFIELD

M & W B

M TRUSTWORTHY

MAPPIN & WEBB'S PRINCE'S PLATE.

MAPPIN & WEBB
ROYAL CUTLERY WORKS, SHEFFIELD & LONDON

TM

MARPLES, T
SHEFFIELD

HIBERNIA

"HIBERNIA"

MARPLES, WILLIAM & SONS
SHEFFIELD

A.H

MARTIN BROTHERS & CO
SHEFFIELD

MH AC

RM EH

MARTIN, HALL & CO
SHREWSBURY WORKS, SHEFFIELD

NEW CALEDONIAN SILVER

MARTINO, F R
BIRMINGHAM

SOUTHERN CROSS BRAND

MASON BROTHERS, LTD
LONDON

TRADE MARK

MATHER, WILLIAM
MANCHESTER

TRADE MARK

MAW, S, SON & THOMPSON
LONDON

1847—ROGERS BROS.—A 1

MERIDEN BRITANNIA CO
LONDON

MERZBACH, LANG & FELLHEIMER
LONDON

MEYERSTEIN, WILLIAM & CO
LONDON

MILNER, WILLIAM & SONS
LEEK

MOENICH, OSCAR & CO
LONDON

S.MORDAN & Cº

MORDAN, S & CO
LONDON

EMPRESS BUTTERFLY

MORETON, JOHN & CO
WOLVERHAMPTON, SHEFFIELD & LONDON

J. M. & Cº

MORTON, JOHN & CO
SHEFFIELD & LONDON

WM

MORTON, W
SHEFFIELD

H.B MUIR & Cº
LONDON

MUIR, H B & CO
LONDON

MUIRHEAD, JAMES & CO
GLASGOW

PYRO GOLD
NEAL'S
PYRO SILVER

NEAL, JOHN & CO
LONDON

JN

NEEDHAM, J
SHEFFIELD

TAYLOR
WITNESS SHEFFIELD
WITNESS

NEEDHAM, VEALL & TYZACK
EYE WITNESS WORKS, SHEFFIELD

A1

NEWTON, ELLIS
BIRMINGHAM

NEWTON, FRANCIS & SONS
PORTOBELLO WORKS, SHEFFIELD

TRADE MARK THE DAISY

NEWTON, FREDERICK & CO
LONDON

JOHN NODDER & SONS OSMINIUM SHEFFIELD

NODDER, JOHN & SON
SHEFFIELD

JN

NORTH, J
SHEFFIELD

NOWILL, JOHN & SONS
SHEFFIELD

O'CONNOR, PATRICK
LANCASHIRE

RAINBOW

OPENSHAW & COMPANY
BIRMINGHAM & LONDON

O&E

OSBORN & ELLIOT
SHEFFIELD

I O

OXLEY, JOHN
SHEFFIELD

PP & Cº

PADLEY, PARKIN & CO
SHEFFIELD

PADLEY, WILLIAM & SON
SHEFFIELD

TRADE MARK WP
WP SILVERITE & C
BOLIVIAN SILVER

PAGE, WILLIAM & CO
BIRMINGHAM

XL ALL
P&M WP

PARKIN & MARSHALL
TELEGRAPH WORKS, SHEFFIELD

PS & Cº

PADLEY, STANIFORTH & CO
SHEFFIELD

PAYTON & COMPANY
BIRMINGHAM

A & F Pears

PEARS, A & F
LONDON & MIDDLESEX

AUTOMATON
Invisible Action
W. E. W.
AMERICAN SILVER ALLOY

PERRY & COMPANY, LTD
BIRMINGHAM

PHOSPHOR BRONZE COMPANY LIMITED
VULCAN.
DURO METAL.
PHOSPHOR.

PHOSPHOR BRONZE CO
SOUTHWARK, SURREY

J.P PARAGON METAL & Cº
P

PINDER, JAMES & CO
COLONIAL PLATE WORKS, SHEFFIELD

Piston Freezing Machine and Ice Company.

PISTON FREEZING MACHINE & ICE CO
MIDDLESEX

TRADE MARK

PLANTERS' STORES & AGENCY CO
LONDON

PLATNAUER BROTHERS
BRISTOL

ELECTRO-POTOSI
POTOSI SILVER EQUAL TO SILVER
POTOSI SILVER

POTOSI, THE COMPANY
BIRMINGHAM

SILVA

POTTER, JOHN HENRY
SHEFFIELD

MP PRIME

PRIME, THOMAS & SON
BIRMINGHAM

WW

PRINGLE, ROBERT & CO
WILDERNESS WORKS, MIDDLESEX

PT

PRYOR, TZACK & CO
SHEFFIELD

RABONE RABONE BROTHERS & Co

RABONE BROTHERS & CO
BIRMINGHAM

WHITE AS SILVER MORE DURABLE IN WEAR
W.R SILVERO & Co

RAE, WILLIAM & CO
LIVERPOOL

I SERVE

RAMSBOTTOM, WALTER J
VINE WORKS, SHEFFIELD

TRADE MARK
INDIAN SAND GOLD

READING, N C & CO
BIRMINGHAM

GOLD LINED
VENETIA GOLD PLATE

READING, N C & CO
BIRMINGHAM (continued)

REID, GEORGE & CO
LONDON

RB

RHODES BROTHERS
SHEFFIELD

A J R

RHODES, JEHOIADA ALSOP
BRITAIN WORKS, SHEFFIELD

VALOR
THEOPHILUS RICHARDS & Co.

RICHARDS, THEOPHILUS & CO
BIRMINGHAM

CHAMPION

RICHARDS, THOMAS S & CO
BIRMINGHAM

RR

RICHARDSON, RICHARD
CORNWALL WORKS, SHEFFIELD

RAINBOW

RIDAL, JOHN
PAXTON WORKS, SHEFFIELD

RIDGE, JOSEPH
SHEFFIELD

THA

RIDGE, WOODCOCK & HARDY
SHEFFIELD

R&B R&B
SYLFERET. SR CB

ROBERTS & BELK
FURNIVAL WORKS, SHEFFIELD

R&B

ROBERTS & BRIGGS
SHEFFIELD

R&H

ROBERTS & HALL
SHEFFIELD

JR

ROBERTS, J
SHEFFIELD

R&S

ROBERTS & SLATER
SHEFFIELD

ER TR

ROBINSON & COMPANY
SHEFFIELD

HIGGINSON ROBINSON
HR
LIVERPOOL

ROBINSON, HIGGINSON
LIVERPOOL

RODGERS' ORIGINAL GENUINE PLATE

RODGERS'

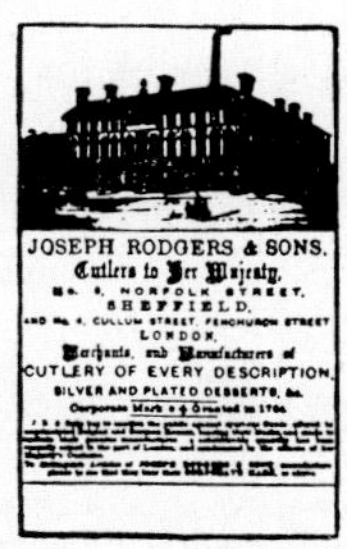
JOSEPH RODGERS & SONS.
Cutlers to Her Majesty.
No. 6, NORFOLK STREET, SHEFFIELD,
LONDON.
CUTLERY OF EVERY DESCRIPTION.
SILVER AND PLATED DESSERTS, &c.

V R
JOSEPH RODGERS & SONS
CUTLERS TO HER MAJESTY
No. 6 NORFOLK ST SHEFFIELD

J RODGERS & SONS

No 6
NORFOLK
STREET
SHEFFIELD

JOSEPH RODGERS & SONS
CUTLERS TO THEIR MAJESTIES
No 6 NORFOLK STREET
SHEFFIELD

V R
JOSEPH RODGERS & SONS
CUTLERS TO HER MAJESTY.

JOSEPH RODGERS

RODGERS, JOSEPH & SONS
SHEFFIELD

RODGERS
CUTLERS
TO HER
MAJESTY

ORIGINAL & GENUINE PLATE

RODGERSINE

JOSEPH RODGERS & SONS

RODGERS JR JR

JR

RODGERS, JOSEPH & SONS
SHEFFIELD (continued)

ROGERS, HENRY & SONS CO
SHEFFIELD & WOLVERHAMPTON

AMAZONE

ROSING

ROSING BROTHERS & CO
LONDON

VICTORY

VICTORY
HENRY ROSSELL & Co
SHEFFIELD.

ROSSELL, HENRY & CO
SHEFFIELD

JOHN ROUND & SON
SHEFFIELD

JR & S EP

VALARIUM

KENDULAM

J.R & S World

ROUND, JOHN & SON, LTD
TUDOR & ARUNDEL WORKS, SHEFFIELD

KENSINGTON

DERBY

Orovide

ROWE, CHARLES COURTNEY
MIDDLESEX

TR

ROYLE, T
SHEFFIELD

SHEFFIELD
RELIABLE
PLATE

RYLAND, WILLIAM
GATEFIELD WORKS, SHEFFIELD

H SAMUEL

TRADE MARK
THE BEST IMITATION OF FINE GOLD KNOWN
BAVARIAN GOLD

SAMUEL, H & SONS
MANCHESTER

S&C

S & C

SANSOM & CRESWICK
SHEFFIELD

The NATIONAL

SAVAGE, W S & CO
SHEFFIELD

OSIRIS

HERMANN SCHURHOFF & Co

ADELANTE

H S

SCHURHOFF, H & CO
BIRMINGHAM

S.S.& Co
London
Sheffield
M.S.Jo&Co

SELIG, SONNENTHAL & CO
LONDON

J.S.& S.

Common Sense

SHAW, JOHN & SONS, LTD
WOLVERTON

S F

SHAW & FISHER
SHEFFIELD

REGENT SILVER

SHERWOOD, JOHN & SONS
BIRMINGHAM

TOTTENHAM HOUSE
1872

SCHOOLBRED, JAMES & CO
MIDDLESEX

A M S

SILBER & FLEMING, LTD
LONDON

THOS BARCLAY & SON

LONDON

SILVERSTON, ISAAC & CO
BIRMINGHAM

WS
GS

WS

SISSONS, WILLIAM & GEORGE
SHEFFIELD & LONDON

SB

SLACK BROTHERS
LEICESTER WORKS, SHEFFIELD

ONWARD

BON-ACCORD

SLACK & GRINOLD
BATH WORKS, SHEFFIELD

VENTURE

SLATER BROTHERS
SHEFFIELD

J·H·S

SLATER, J & SON
SHEFFIELD

S & H

SLATER, SON & HORTON
SHEFFIELD

SMITH, CHARLES
SHEFFIELD

JS

SMITH, JOSEPHUS
SHEFFIELD

ALFE NIDE

SOCIETE ANONYME DES CONVERTS ALFENIDE
PARIS

KANGAROO

SORBY, ROBERT & SONS
SHEFFIELD

SPENCER SHEFFIELD
NIMROD
MATTHIAS SPENCER & SONS

SPENCER, MATTHIAS & SONS
SHEFFIELD

HERALD
TRUMPETER

SPEYER, C A E & CO
LONDON

SPEYER, SCHWERDT & CO
LONDON

GORDON SILVER

SPURRIER & COMPANY
LONDON

Everlasting

STACEY BROTHERS
SHEFFIELD

S & H

STACEY, HENRY & HORTON
SHEFFIELD

STANIFORTH, WILLIAM T
ASCEND WORKS, SHEFFIELD

The Steam Electro-Plating and Gilding Company

STEAM ELECTRO-PLATING & G CO
SOUTHAMPTON

W S H S

STRATFORD, W & H
SHEFFIELD

MIXITINE

SWANN & ADAMS
CANADA WORKS, BIRMINGHAM

EUREKA

HAY, WILLIAM
BIRMINGHAM

TAYLOR BROTHERS
ADELAIDE WORKS, SHEFFIELD

TRADE MARK W.R.H.

TAYLOR & COMPANY
SWANSEA

GT

TEASDELL, G
LONDON

T & B

THOMPSON & BROWN
SHEFFIELD

JT J.T

THOMPSON, J
SHEFFIELD

THORNHILL, WALTER
MIDDLESEX

MEXICAN SILVER

TIDMARSH, JAMES
LONDON

TIMM, F E
SHEFFIELD

LIFE

TOWNSEND, FRANCIS JOHN
SHEFFIELD

J.T T.T

TOWNDROW BROTHERS
SHEFFIELD

T.T

TURNER, THOMAS
SHEFFIELD

T.T

TURNER, THOMAS & CO
SUFFOLK WORKS, SHEFFIELD

GU

UNITE, G
BIRMINGHAM

TRADE MARK

VAN WART, SON & CO
BIRMINGHAM

VERNON, JAMES & BROTHER
WIGTOWN

LONDON

VERNON'S PATENT CHINA & GLASS CO, LTD
LONDON

THE HOPE PLATE
TRADE MARK

VIVIAN, H H & CO, LTD
BIRMINGHAM

VON DER MEDEN, CARL A
LONDON

W&H
H HALL.
PALACE SILVER
SONORA SILVER
W&H

WALKER & HALL
SHEFFIELD

WK &Cº

WALKER, KNOWLES & CO
SHEFFIELD

THE GREAT EASTERN

WALSHAM, R & J
BIRMINGHAM

IXION

WALTON, G E & CO, LTD
BIRMINGHAM

GW

WARD, GEORGE
SHEFFIELD

SW

WARD, W & S
MANCHESTER

W&Cº W&S

WATERHOUSE, GEORGE & CO
SHEFFIELD

WELLS, GALLIMORE & TAYLOR
BIRMINGHAM

WHEELER, GEORGE
BIRMINGHAM

W W & J H

WHITE, HENDERSON & CO
ELCHO WORKS, SHEFFIELD

WW TJ

WHITE & JOHNSTONE
SHEFFIELD

WHITE & RIDSDALE
LONDON

TRADE MARK THE SQUIRREL

WHITE, THOMAS
BIRMINGHAM

Imperial F.W.

Electro-Imperial F.W.

Imperial Silver F.W.

WHITEHOUSE, FREDERICK
LION WORKS, BIRMINGHAM

TRADE MARK WILLIAM WHITELEY UNIVERSAL PROVIDER WESTBOURNE GROVE LONDON W.

UNIVERSAL PROVIDER.

WHITELEY, WILLIAM
MIDDLESEX

DEFIANCE

WILKIN, GEORGE
PALMERSTON WORKS, SHEFFIELD

HW &CO

NEILL NEILL

WILKINSON, HENRY & CO, LTD
SHEFFIELD

WILKINSON, T & SONS
BIRMINGHAM

ACME.

WILLIAMSON, HENRY
LONDON

WILSON, JOHN
SHEFFIELD

FW WD

W & D L & S

W & D S BP

WILSON & DAVIS
LONDON & SHEFFIELD

2216

WINTER, ROBERT
SHEFFIELD

BOVAL

WOOLLEY, JAMES, SONS & CO
MANCHESTER

WOSTENHOLM, G & SON, LTD
WASHINGTON WORKS, SHEFFIELD

I XL

WOSTENHOLME, J
SHEFFIELD

J.W

W.F.W

WOSTENHOLME, W F
SHEFFIELD

YATES'S VIRGINIAN SILVER

SILVEN

NICKELOID

YATES, JOHN & SONS
BIRMINGHAM

Y & S

J Y & S

YATES & SONS

J. YATES & SONS

JOHN YATES & SONS

YATES VIRGINIAN SILVER

Y

V S

J Y & S

J Y & S

J YATES & SONS

SILVURN

SILVERN

SILVERN

YATES'S VIRGINIAN

SILVER ASH

YATES, JOHN & SONS
BIRMINGHAM (continued)

YORK, SAMUEL & CO
WOLVERHAMPTON

ELECTROPLATING

The electroplating process of covering a metal article with a coating of pure silver was perfected by Elkington & Co of Birmingham. This procedure rapidly adopted by the silver industry in Britain and other parts of the world during the early 1840s.

The method of electroplating has not changed from that time to the present day. A Portland cement-lined vat is the vessel into which a solution of potassium cyanide is poured. The vat must be scrupulously clean for the electroplating process to work successfully. The presence of dirt causes imperfections to appear on the finished article. A low voltage current is then passed through the liquid with the positive pole attached to a silver sheet and the negative pole attached to the article to be plated, a teapot, for example. The silver sheet is a cathode and its pure particles pass from the dissolving sheet onto the teapot. Once plated, the teapot is hammered all over, to ensure adhesion of the coating, and then burnished. Electrogilding (gold-plating) is done in exactly the same way.

This method is a distinct improvement on the earlier process of mercury gilding, where the release of poisonous fumes interfered with health and shortened the life expectancy of workers exposed to them.

A variety of base metals can be used for eletroplating. Copper and nickel or a combination of both have proved to be the most satisfactory. Brass and Britannia base metal (see glossary) were commonly used in earlier times. This latter amalgam was cheap to produce and used extensively throughout America and, to a lesser extent, Britain. It was considered inferior because its softness made it less durable; it was difficult to repair or replate and finished articles lacked the fine lustre of those made with other base metals. It is recommended, therefore, that electro-formed articles having a Britannia metal base are only purchased for ornamental purposes.

The introduction of electroplating led to the swift demise of Old Sheffield Plate production, leaving only a handful of companies still making articles of fused plate. Even these ceased to use the fusion method within 10 years of the advent of electroplate. The labour-intensive and complex construction of fused plate had been acceptable while silver was an expensive commodity and the workforce was cheap to employ. However, during the early 1800s came a change in fortunes and the price difference between a sterling silver piece and an Old Sheffield one narrowed considerably. Only electroplate offered a truly economic alternative.

The rush to change to this new manufacturing method meant that many companies were obliged to scrap existing machines and tooling to finance the new equipment needed for electroplating. It offered many advantages over the fused process. The article to be plated was first cast in the base metal and then plated, as opposed to being worked from a

ABOVE
Silver plated condiment set. A detail of the registration mark is on page 73.

LEFT
A brass and silver plated table bell.

LEFT
A Britannia base metal biscuit box. The silver has been completely worn away exposing the dull grey base underneath.

fused and rolled ingot. It could be decorated with applied metal mounts, instead of costly silver ones, and there was no longer a need to fill the mounts with lead as reinforcement. The amount of silver used on an electroplated article was negligible and the labour cost cut in half. The end product was both durable and pleasing to the buying public. The popularity of silverware was growing as a result of increased wealth enjoyed by a larger segment of society.

Electroplated silver articles have stronger soldered joints than their fused counterparts. Old Sheffield articles were soldered with soft lead, which has a tendency to break. Repairs to fused silver are difficult in any case but in addition the smallest amount of heat applied will quickly spread through the article and melt the lead present in the mounts and joins on the body. Most electroplating articles (except those containing Britannia base metal) are soldered with an amalgam of silver and nickel, known as hard solder, which gives a stronger and more permanent join.

Articles for electroplating could be engraved first, whereas it was not possible to engrave Old Sheffield at all, without letting-in a heavier silver insert, eliminating the exposure of copper beneath. Techniques previously used only on sterling silver were suitable for electroplate, allowing the variety of articles produced to increase dramatically.

One disadvantage of electroplating, however, is that the pure silver surface, being softer than the sterling silver finish on Old Sheffield Plate, wears much more quickly. Replating is therefore a not uncommon requirement; fortunately, this is inexpensive. Another disadvantage of electroplate is that it never achieves the patina of sterling silver. Because it is pure silver its colour is whiter and therefore differs from that of sterling silver and fused plate.

ABOVE
Machine-embossed section of a silver plated biscuit box. Unlike hand-engraving, machine-embossed decorations have a pressed-in appearance. Also noticeable are the fine exact lines incorporated in the pattern work. The embossing may show through faintly on the inside, but not in the same manner as hand-chasing which will show pattern definition quite clearly.

RIGHT
A section of a machine-embossed tray, revealing the same fine lines within the pattern as that on the biscuit box. Because the machine press or roller was not applied with sufficient pressure, the central pattern highlights are faded and in some sections have not made an imprint at all.

Electro-Forming

A spin-off of the invention of electroplating was electro-forming or electro-typing. Also developed in 1840, this is a method of moulding an article that can then be electroplated.

Metal is deposited on the inside of a shaped mould in particles, using the same basic procedure as electroplating. The metal is removed when sufficient has been deposited to give the desired thickness. The mould is made of gutta-percha, a gum from the Malayan Percha tree, and is usually elaborately detailed. The formed articles can then be electro-silvered or gold-plated and finished in the usual way.

Electro-forming has advantages over other casting methods. Minimal shrinkage occurs, the silver is not porous, close control can be kept of the metal deposited, and it is the only process that enables both engraving and chasing to be accomplished at the same time. Its development was considered important because it allowed intricate items – made from inexpensive base metals instead of silver or gold – to be produced at a fraction of the cost of handmade articles. Not just the metal price but also the labour costs were reduced, as earlier detailed articles had been labour-intensive to manufacture.

The invention of electro-forming led to the widespread reproduction of world-famous works of art and silverware housed in museum collections. Items from the Imperial Russian Collection were copied in the 1890s and sent to educational establishments for teaching purposes.

Elkington, who perfected electro-forming, hired the finest artists of the day to produce designs inspired by early civilizations. Prominent examples include the Milton shield, designed by Leonard Morel-Ladeuil, (now in the Victoria and Albert Museum in London), which won a gold medal at the Paris Exhibition of 1867, and a ewer by François Briot, based on a 16th-century original.

Elkington & Co licensed, among others, Christofle of France, to use both electro-processes. To the present day, Christofle has operated successfully, producing goods to a very high standard. Elkington, on the other hand, went into a decline between the two World Wars and was eventually sold off. The name was bought by another silversmith, but the quality silverware that was the Elkington hallmark is no longer made. At present, there are a number of English and American companies producing electroplate hollow ware of reasonable quality, but, because labour costs are now exorbitant, little or no fine hand-decorations are undertaken, leaving small incentive to purchase new pieces.

By contrast, some new English flatware is still produced to a very high standard, comparable to electroplate produced in previous times. Companies producing superior flatware have their own pattern dies and use heavy gauge blanks (the base over which each piece is electro-silver plated). A heavier gauge means the blank can be struck harder without bending or breaking. This type of flatware is very well finished and each item carries a heavy deposit of silver, ensuring many years of functional use.

When checking whether or not a piece is electro-formed, look for the tell-tale nodular effect on shield backs and on the interior of hollow ware pieces. In addition, shields are sometimes backed with lead, although this is not always visible, as many were finished with sheet metal using conventional manufacturing methods.

One of the most frequently asked questions is "are there hallmarks on electro-silver plated articles?". The answer is no. The only marks permitted on electroplate are manufacturers' marks that are not permitted to resemble hallmarks. Some makers put on marks that, when put into a similar sequence to hallmarks, might at first glance look like a hallmark. Closer inspection will reveal this is not the case. Only silver is allowed to be hallmarked.

Registry Marks

Between 1842 and 1883 the British Patent Office used a Registry mark on British manufactured goods. The mark shows the exact year, month and date of an object. The year letters run in a sequence from 1842 to 1867 as follows: X, H, C, A, I, F, U, S, V, P, D, Y, J, E, L, K, B, M, Z, R, O, G, N, W, Q, T. In 1868 the mark was changed slightly and the sequence ran from X in 1868 to K in 1883. The months were indicated by the letters C, G, W, H, E, M, I, R, D, B, K, A. R was used for 1st–19th September 1857, K for December 1860, and G for 1st–6th March 1878, the latter with W for the year.

From 1884 to 1900 serial numbers were used on registered designs. The first numbers in each year were as follows: 1884 1; 1885 19754; 1886 40480; 1887 64520; 1888 90483; 1889 11648; 1890 141273; 1891 163767; 1892 185713; 1893 205240; 1894 224720; 1895 246975; 1896 268392; 1897 291241; 1898 311658; 1899 331707; 1900 351202.

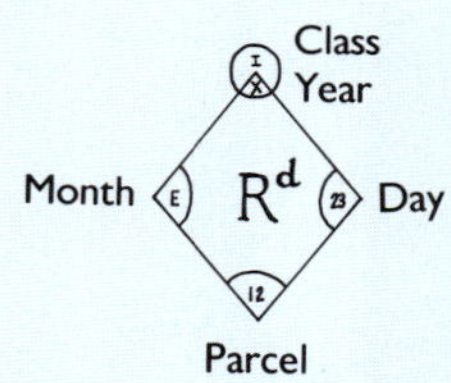

Registry mark used between 1842 and 1867. This particular one shows the date 23rd March 1842.

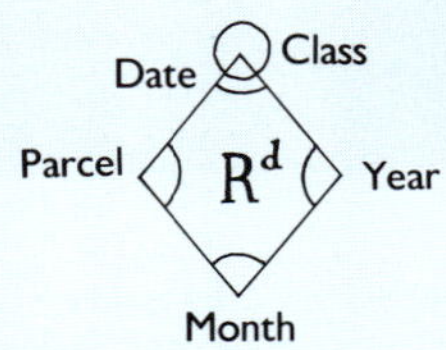

Registry mark for the years 1868–1883.

ABOVE

Electroplated objects are not permitted to have hallmarks. This is a registration mark.

Condition and quality

CONDITION

The condition of any article of sterling silver, Old Sheffield or electroplate, is of paramount importance in trying to establish its worth, both in financial and utilitarian terms. The finest quality antique silver can be reduced to a fraction of its potential value if damaged or abused and can be virtually useless from a practical point of view, whereas high-quality silver that has been well maintained will always be valuable. Condition is all.

The pointers provided in this chapter should help you to decide whether silver already owned or to be acquired is in good condition or not. This section covers significant alterations or additions that affect both condition and quality. This chapter also examines silver articles made for one purpose but later altered to suit another, together with decoration added many years following original manufacture, reflecting changing styles and tastes.

ABOVE

Tankard by Philip Syng Jr, Philadelphia *c.* 1750. A fine example of the silversmith's skill, with domed cover, scroll thumbpiece and moulded footrim.

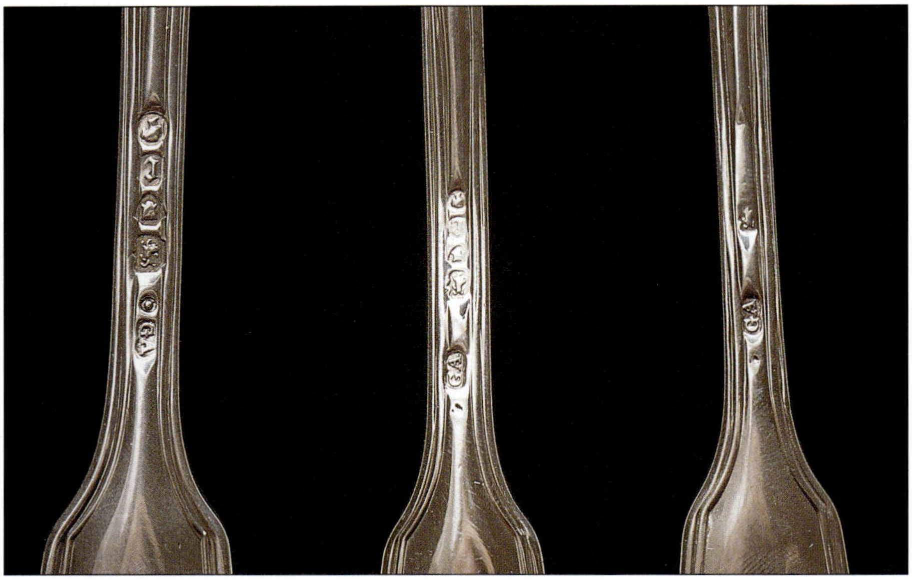

ABOVE

The condition of the hallmark is essential for identifying and dating the piece accurately and usually indicates the overall condition of the article. The hallmark on the left is clear and shows all marks in detail, the hallmark in the centre is acceptable because one can still identify the origin, date and maker, but the hallmark on the right, although showing the maker's mark, has a worn out hallmark and does not give the information needed.

STERLING SILVER

Hallmarks and their importance in establishing the worth and authenticity of silver have already been covered. Suffice it to say that if any article has hallmarks that are worn past the point of recognition by use or excessive polishing, doubt is cast on its overall condition. Although American articles are not hallmarked, worn maker's marks would also contribute to a lessening of an article's value. When assessing condition, also look at any decorations such as engraving or chased work. If the work looks crisp and well defined and the hallmarks are clear, then these are good indications of the overall state of the piece.

Don't stop too soon; continue your examination to ensure that the hallmarks on any attached lids, handles, etc match those on the base. Because a maker's mark is usually only placed on the main body of American silverware, this only applies to English goods. Hold hollow ware such as teapots and soup tureens up to the light to check for pinholes and cracks, and do the same with trays and salvers. Look out for splits and cracks on handles, borders and spouts.

Push gently with your thumb or the palm of your hand against the sides and centres of articles to ascertain whether an object is generally too thin or worn in patches. Thinness is determined by the amount of 'give' felt. If you are considering a purchase, ask the owner's permission first, as a heavy-handed approach to a thin surface could cause a section to cave in, causing a difficult and embarrassing situation. If you would prefer not to undertake this test yourself, ask the owner to do it and watch very carefully. Make sure silver trays are of a reasonable thickness for weight-bearing. This is particularly important as sterling silver is not flexible. Once it is bent, it *stays* bent.

Look out for 'blacksmiths' repairs', so called because, in the past, many crude repairs were carried out in the country by the village smith. This was usually due to the distant location of the nearest silversmith and the difficulty of travel. These repairs, whether to a broken foot or handle, or the reinforcement of a leaking spout, can be detected very easily. Look at articles, both inside and out, checking for grey uneven patches around spouts, handles, seams, hinges, feet and bases. This lack of smoothness and discoloration is usually lead solder and indicates a 'blacksmith's repair'.

Items that have become thin or worn through are sometimes patched by soldering another piece of silver onto or into the worn section. In most cases these patches can be seen quite easily by examining the inside of the objects – or on salvers and trays, the underneath – for the outline of the patch. Sometimes a patch can be clearly seen sitting proud on top of a surface. Chased decoration added at a later date often distorts the hallmark, affecting both quality and condition. Such chasing can also cause thin spots by stretching the metal.

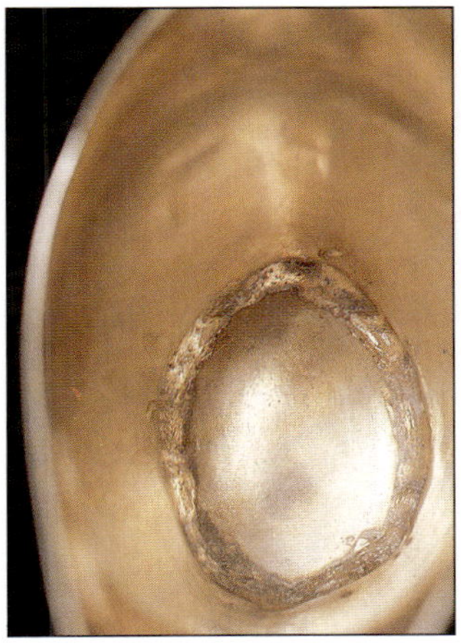

ABOVE

A cream jug which, on close inspection, appears in very poor condition.

LEFT

The cream jug shows a band of etching and engraving that looks jaded; this is due to excessive wear, and is an indication that the piece will be rather worn overall.

TOP LEFT

An interior view showing a repair to the base, almost certainly necessitated by leakage.

This silver jug made around 1795, at a time when silver was at a premium, started life as a rather thin piece, and its delicate nature and rough treatment has led to its ruination.

TOP RIGHT

The same cream jug, showing a crude repair where the handle meets the body.

REMEDIES FOR STERLING

If you own silver that you think is in need of restoration, it is important to find a proper silversmith, specializing in restoration, to undertake the work. These smiths are hard to find, as only a handful remain who have the necessary tools and expertise to carry out successful repair work. Repairs should enhance the piece rather than further destroy its beauty or value.

When you find a specialist restorer, obtain a quote for doing a first-rate job and then decide if the article is worth the work. Good restoration can bring an item in poor condition back to near-perfection, but a great deal of money can be spent in the process. Only an expert silver dealer or restorer can advise whether or not restoration is worthwhile. If the article has great sentimental value then the choice becomes easier and more subjective.

Never buy a piece in need of repair in the hope that restoration will increase its worth and usefulness unless you are quite certain of the cost of the repairs. When buying from an auction house or a dealer, you must ask yourself why the vendor has not already had the repairs carried out.

The condition of cutlery can be established quite easily with a few simple tests. One of the first checks to make is whether or not the pieces are usable and will stand up to regular use. Fork prongs should be sturdy and straight rather than too thin and prone to bending. They should be long and elegantly proportioned in relation to the total size of the fork, not stubby looking, and make sure that there are no signs of drastically uneven wear. The shanks of forks should be thick enough to withstand downward pressure without bending and spoons should also have thick shanks, as well as bowls. Again, spoon bowls should not show uneven wear nor should they have thin or sharp

LEFT
Fiddle pattern tablespoon in worn condition. The thin bowl, now distorted, is clearly visible. By running a finger around the edge of the bowl one can feel an unacceptable sharpness.

BELOW
Two silver bead pattern dessert spoons. The second article shows extensive wear to the pattern.

ABOVE LEFT
Rear view of an Old English pattern tablespoon showing a patch repair. This indicates that the spoon has become thin and cracked during usage.

ABOVE RIGHT
Two table forks, one with prongs in perfect condition, the other worn down and thin. To test the quality press gently against the end of the prongs.

ABOVE
A bead pattern dessert fork with heavily worn prongs that are unacceptably short and thin, rendering the article almost useless.

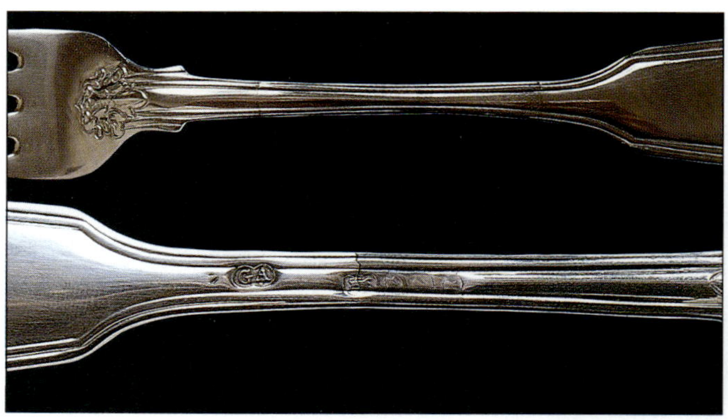

TOP
A fiddle thread and husk pattern dessert fork which has suffered serious misuse and has been repaired. Notice the two hairline cracks where rejoining has been attempted.

BOTTOM
This dessert fork from the same set shows a hairline crack as well as a worn out hallmark illustrating the overall poor condition.

TOP LEFT AND BELOW LEFT
Queen's pattern dessert spoons, front and back view. The article on the bottom shows crisp well-defined detailing on the pattern and a clear hallmark whereas the article on the top has worn decorations and an almost unrecognizable hallmark.

LEFT
Bright cut engraved dessert spoon and fork. The fork has level prongs that are strong and of a good length, as well as sharply defined engraving, whereas the spoon decoration is faded in sections.

edges. When pressed or flexed gently, they should feel solid and not yield to the point where you feel that they will bend.

Next, look at the pattern of the cutlery, if any, to check that it is not worn away in parts, then ensure that the hallmarks are legible. Check prongs and shanks for hairline cracks or fine lines running through. (This will indicate that the piece has been broken and then soldered together again.)

Because the great majority of American flatware is rather thin to begin with, bending will occur without too much pressure. Different criteria apply when examining these pieces – look out for a well-defined pattern and lack of excess wear.

When English or American flatware satisfy these basic requirements, they can generally be said to be in good condition.

OLD SHEFFIELD/FUSED PLATE

The methods of ascertaining the condition of Old Sheffield Plate are quite different from those employed for sterling silver. The original construction process differs from that of sterling, with lead solder used for almost every join, the intricate and labour-intensive assembly of a number of components to create a whole, and many articles with tinned interiors and undersides making it hard to spot later repairs.

It is better to own or acquire Old Sheffield articles that have not been electroplated, as this process diminishes their value and interest. Electroplating is often carried out when the object becomes worn and excessive copper is exposed. It is not always easy to spot replated articles with the untrained eye. Silversmiths can impose a dull lustre onto newly replated silver, accurately simulating the appearance of Old Sheffield Plate.

Original Old Sheffield items will usually show slight wear, revealing a little copper on proud areas. Known in the trade as 'bleeding', this is perfectly acceptable and even desirable.

Most decorations applied to surface edges were made of thin silver and then filled with lead solder to give additional strength. With age and use the silver can be worn away, exposing the lead underneath. If you can spot excessive lead on the edges this is not a good sign and indicates a rather tired article. The borders should show crisp detail and no sign

Urns usually have tinned interiors, as do most articles of Old Sheffield hollow ware. This dark grey surface is perfectly serviceable, even though the appearance is not visually attractive. All urns have a large lump of solder in evidence around the inside join where the spigot is attached, the device which controls the flow of liquid. This is not a sign of restoration, just the means of securing a strong joint. However, if there is solder around the spigot on the outside, this does indicate a later repair.

This rule is applicable for any items of Old Sheffield hollow ware – solder on the outside is indicative of restoration, solder on the inside or underside a manufacturing technique; the principle being that if it didn't show, it didn't matter. Old Sheffield was, after all, referred to as 'poor man's silver' although in comparison with articles made by today's electroplate methods, Old Sheffield must be considered the work of the gods!

RIGHT

A 'Blacksmith's' repair to the handle and body of an Old Sheffield Plate coffee pot. The lead solder is clearly visible and whereas it may last for quite a while, it is extremely unsightly, and severely diminishes the value.

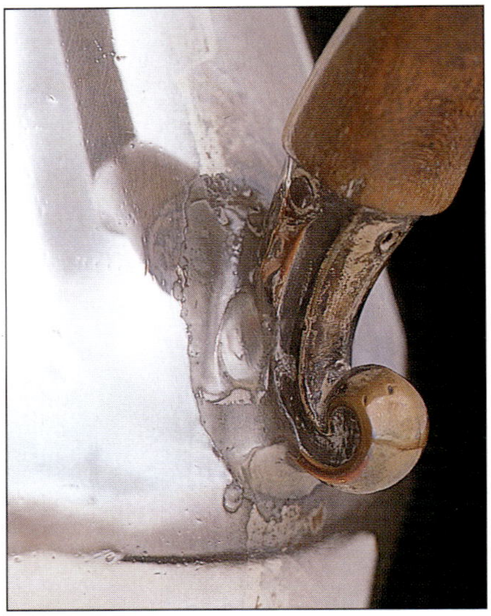

BELOW RIGHT

This spout repair has been reasonably well concealed although the lead solder around the top of the spout is visible.

BELOW

A reinforcing silver L-shaped piece has been soldered underneath the handle of a cream jug that had been split at the join. When it was originally made, there never would have been a strengthening piece applied in this manner, thereby indicating a repair.

RIGHT

A section of an Old Sheffield Plate coaster where the silver has been almost completely removed through excessive polishing, exposing the copper on the body and the lead beneath the applied silver border.

ABOVE

The side profile of an Old Sheffield Plate coaster. The joining seam has come away. There is also a patch beneath the rim which at some point has been applied to prevent separation.

It is always important to examine each part of every article to establish not only the condition, but also all the interesting aspects to be found in Old Sheffield hollow ware. High-quality items, often made for the aristocracy, were fitted with let-in shields. Apart from these shields, finer articles often have detachable parts that are hallmarked sterling silver, such as custom-made finials or handles on entrée dishes or meat-dish covers. Sometimes the 'bottons' (discs) fixed to the centre of the wood bases of bottle and decanter coasters are hallmarked sterling, while having Old Sheffield frames. Occasionally, larger articles are a combination of Old Sheffield and sterling silver pieces to cut down to on the overall cost. For instance, the cover of an entrée dish may be made of sterling silver but the warming base may be made of Old Sheffield Plate.

The condition of close-plating – the covering of steel with sterling silver usually associated with flatware or scissor-type candle snuffers – is quite easy to identify. Fusing silver to steel has not proven satisfactory in the long term; the construction process usually leads to rust underneath the silver surface. Little can be done to halt this corrosion, which can usually be seen as bubbles of rust; very few articles are free of it. As one would expect, the degree of corrosion determines the overall condition and ultimate value.

ELECTROPLATE

Once again, a different set of criteria apply when checking the condition of electroplate. The variety of base metals used, some durable, others not so, determines the usefulness of an electroplate article.

For example, a coffee pot containing copper or nickel, the most successful base metals, will be much more durable than one made with Britannia base metal, a soft alloy which looks good but costs little, produced to fill a demand at the lower end

of the market. Soft-base metal (ie Britannia metal) was much favoured by American manufacturers. Therefore, when purchasing it is essential to ensure that the piece is not in need of restoration or replating. Both will be difficult to accomplish.

As with sterling silver and Old Sheffield Plate, leaks and repairs will be visible around the exterior of the body, but, unlike Old Sheffield, any repairs to the interior will be quite easy to spot. The nature of the manufacturing process means that all surfaces should be plated with silver. The interiors may not be polished to a bright finish but will be quite smooth and easily recognizable as silver.

Thin sides are not usually a problem arising with electroplate. Sterling silver articles with thin patches are often the result of filing and/or polishing by heavy-handed silversmiths to remove initials or crests from shields or carouche decorations. In contrast, copper and nickel are very tough and can take a great deal of punishment, though Britannia metal is so soft that any attempt to remove inscriptions on an article would hole the side. Also, where hard-base metal was used on the main body of the article, soft metal (ie Britannia metal) was often used to make added decorative mounts, handles and/or supports. These were an inherent weakness when the items were in regular use.

When considering a purchase, look to see if there are any written indications to describe the base metal used. There are three marks of confirmation but their use is not compulsory. The marks and their translations are:

EPBM – electroplated Britannia metal
EPCN – electroplated copper/nickel amalgem
EPNS – electroplated nickel silver

NB: A1 appearing on electroplate does not denote any particular standard. It was used as a sales ploy to insinuate quality. American makers often stated 'Hard metal' on their wares, to denote copper or nickel base metals.

You can do your own test to establish the metal base of silver other than sterling. Britannia metal can be tested by tapping the object against a ring on your finger; if it contains Britannia metal, a dull resonance is heard, rather than a clear ringing sound.

Other base metals can be identified by taking a file or sharp knife and, very carefully, exposing the tiniest amount of base metal in an inconspicuous place. If the metal revealed is grey-coloured, it is nickel; Britannia base metal shows as blackish-grey, and copper as a distinctive pink-orange hue. It should be stressed that this method is for home use only and would be unacceptable in any silver showroom.

Although much fine decorative handiwork can be found lavished on Britannia metal goods, especially in the United

TOP

From left to right: An Old Sheffield Plate wax jack *c.* 1800.
A close up of the collapsed border.
A close-up of uneven solder work indicating a repair.
A close-up of a good repair.

ABOVE

A side profile of an Old Sheffield Plate coaster, showing exposed copper base metal.

LEFT

A nickel and silver-plated water jug in need of re-plating.

LEFT

These two silver-plated pieces of flatware show unacceptable levels of wear with worn prongs on the fork and exposed nickel highlights on the underside of the ladle bowl and shank. When inspecting plated flatware always look at the underside of the spoons and forks as this is the area most prone to wear.

ABOVE RIGHT

A sterling silver pierced basket made in London in 1896.

RIGHT

Detail of the hand-pierced fret work and hand engraving, as well as the cast and hand-chased border.

States, the life expectancy of such items is not high, since Britannia metal was produced to supply affordable goods for the less affluent. As mentioned before, this base metal melts at a very low temperature, which dictates that any repairs can only be rudimentary. It dents very easily, does not hold its plate surface well and is extremely hard to replace.

Many people inherit impressive-looking heirlooms containing Britannia base metal only to find that if used regularly they are difficult to maintain. They are often best kept in showcases to be admired but not used. This is not true of the hand-decorated articles made with a durable copper or nickel base, which frequently have wonderful chasing and engraving, as well as finely cast applied mounts and ornaments. These were made to last, and do.

On all electroplate items, check that the decorations are sharp and not worn in patches. Any fading and lack of clarity will reduce not just the appearance but the worth. The same applies to chasing-work; rubbed and hazy relief details affect the value.

QUALITY

STERLING SILVER

Defining quality in silverware becomes a relative assessment. Taking sterling silver articles made in 1770 and comparing them with similar objects produced 100 years later might tell us that technical innovations improved – finish and form on the latter, but the former benefited from the fact that most stages of its manufacture were accomplished by hand. American silversmiths did not 'benefit' from British technical advancements during the Industrial Revolution until several years later, largely because of distance. Therefore the articles produced in the former colonies had much of the idiosyncratic charm of earlier English pieces. It was not until early-to mid-19th century that British technical innovations took hold in America. The resultant lack of uniformity, and the variations in terms of technical merit and aesthetics makes it particularly hard to value American pieces in comparison to their English counterparts.

For the purist collector of fine sterling silver, pre-Industrial Revolution pieces are considered the apogee of the craft. This is because age and rarity make objects desirable and, more importantly, because the silverware was custom-designed and made from start to finish by one person at one workshop. In the post-Industrial Revolution atelier, the creation was initiated by a designer, then produced by a number of specialist craft-workers using a variety of sophisticated techniques, machines and tools. The resultant finished product, therefore, could be copied repeatedly in a uniform fashion.

Concentrating on sterling silver from the 1700s to the early 20th century, the quality of hand decorations, form and weight will now be examined and we will see that with later pieces other factors must also be taken into account.

Where weight is concerned, if two objects of the same type and approximate size are weighed, obviously the heavier of the two is the better, having greater durability. If a piece feels flimsy and light, as though the slightest knock will impair its form or render it unusable, it is likely to be of inferior quality. The photographs and accompanying captions to this chapter will best illustrate the difference between good and poor quality in form and decoration.

During the period 1770–1790, silversmiths produced most of their wares in lighter gauges of metal, as sterling silver was an expensive and heavily taxed commodity. The neo-classic style that dominated this period naturally lent itself to a more economic use of the metal, a fact which should be taken into account when assessing quality. Bright cut engraving was a very popular form of embellishment during the same period,

RIGHT

This presentation cup and cover incorporates excellent hand-chasing around the body and cover and extremely well-defined cast finial.

RIGHT

A detail of a chased section of the cup.

BELOW RIGHT

Interior view of the same section. The yellow colour is gold plating.

BELOW

A superb quality sterling silver tea and coffee service in the style of Teniers made in 1834 by Edward Farrell. The pieces incorporate intricately detailed cast work as well as hand-chased scenes set in high relief. Chasing is a process whereby the decoration is created by hammering the exterior of the article, and by using certain tools a relief is created by 'pinching' the silver.

ABOVE

This illustrates the difference between hand-engraving and machine-embossing. The hand-engraved foliage on the left, although containing a myriad of lines, does not have the pressed in appearance nor the exact geometric evenness of the machine-embossed piece.

RIGHT

A pair of sterling silver cast candlesticks, 1810. These candlesticks, unlike their stamped and filled counter-parts, are of a very heavy gauge silver and therefore are self-supporting. After casting, candlesticks would have been hand-chased to further define the pattern.

TOP

The underside of the candlestick is illustrated.

ABOVE

The detailed section of the base of the candlestick.

as was piercing. Like earlier pieces, hollow ware was hand-raised, so although lighter in weight, it still showed a good amount of handwork.

Pressed and spun hollow ware did not appear until the middle of the 19th century, but stamped patterns were being used to manufacture candlesticks which were thin, hollow forms, filled with tar or pitch to give weight and strength. Cast candlesticks were and still are the bench-mark of good quality, being self-supporting and requiring no filling. The only advantage of using the stamped process was the enormous variety of style and form permutations that were made possible.

To gauge the quality of stamped candlesticks, look at the underside edge, usually covered in felt. If it is paper thin, it is a sign of lesser quality. Now remove the nozzle or wax drip of the candlestick and flex the cylinder that inserts it into the stick. Again, if it is paper-thin and feels as though it will bend without much effort, it is a sign of inferior quality. Remember to look over the entire candlestick for splits or hairline fractures or worn spots, as these early items were prone to such damage.

CUTLERY AND FLATWARE

Prior to the late 17th century, cutlery was handmade. Not much survives, but there are some wonderful examples of

FAR LEFT

A silver wine ewer by Joseph and Albert Savory, 1852. The elegant form incorporates the best aspect of Victorian design with intricately detailed cast and applied masks as well as excellent hand-engraving.

LEFT AND BELOW

Details of hand-engraving and cast of wine ewer.

early eating irons, designed to spoil the fun of eating with fingers! For the most part these spoons and forks were substantial and durable, whereas the knives were not.

The construction of a knife consisted of producing a handle in two parts, soldering it together, and filling it with hot pitch (shellac). The steel blade shank pin was sunk into the pitch, which set, gripping the blade pin. Steel can rust or a blade can wear out. Replacing a blade involves melting the tar to release it and the usual outcome is that the handle collapses in the process. It is only in recent times that technology has been perfected to produce really hard-wearing knives. This is probably the only area of the trade to improve in modern times, but it should be said that improvements in knife-making are due more to the steel industry than to silversmithing.

Before the end of the 17th century, flatware services were virtually unknown in Britain; the French court was where these new civilized eating habits developed. They were then readily adopted by the British in an effort to 'keep up' with their foreign neighbours. The fork, a two-pronged instrument, was used to hold food still whilst cutting it. The use of a knife, fork or spoon in tandem must be considered the beginning of the flatware service as it is known today – spoon forks, knives and serving items of a uniform design. Teaspoons produced during the 18th century were smaller than coffee spoons of the same era. Tea was by far the most expensive commodity of the two and teacups were made half the size of coffee bowls.

The basic service gained more items as time passed, culminating in the unwieldy but magnificent Victorian services, sometimes containing as many as 14 pieces per place setting. A Victorian table laid for a special occasion must have been a sight to behold and no doubt the cause of confusion for many seated at it, with such an array of cutlery at each place.

LEFT

Silver dessert spoon and fork in the Irish bright cut pattern, a style most popular during the 1780s. Both pieces show excellent definition of the pattern, the prongs of the fork are long and even and the spoon bowl shows no sign of wear.

LEFT

Three pieces from a silver gilt dessert service made by Lias Brothers in 1872. The well defined detail of the pattern makes these pieces exceptional.

BELOW LEFT

The various stages that go into creating a hand forged silver spoon.

As far as quality of work is concerned, cutlery made by hand is superior in all respects to that made by machine. The definition of pattern, form and weight will always be better on handmade silver as illustrated in the figure above. Hand-forged silver flatware is still made in Britain and America in small quantities.

The earliest attempts at mass-producing flatware were made by William Darby of Sheffield, who in 1785 patented his invention for mass-stamping the pattern, form and shape of spoons and forks. Very few examples of his production survive, which suggests that these first machine-made articles were not popular with the buying public when first available. Since it was not until the middle of the 19th century that Sheffield silver manufacturers started mass-producing silverware and electroplate, it therefore can be assumed that all or most cutlery made prior to 1840 was handmade. Certainly, until the turn of the 20th century, the majority of flatware manufactured in London was handmade. Mass-production was left to the cities of Sheffield and Birmingham, a situation characteristic of most other categories of silverware.

Many silversmiths found patronage in London. Pieces made there are likely to be of finer quality than anywhere else in Britain, though there are, of course, many exceptions to this rule. Good provincial silversmiths were responsible for numerous wonderful items, but the primacy of London is still taken as a basic against which all other centres are judged.

Birmingham and Sheffield, located in the industrial heartland of Britain, had innovative machinery for mass-production and enlightened workers, providing the new middle classes with a product they could afford. But during the course of the 20th century, the size and weight of machinery has shrunk in the attempt to keep ordinary flatware competitive. This was especially true of American manufacturing. The resulting products are largely devoid of charm, definition and form. Values fluctuate with the rise and fall of silver spot prices, which for some years have been in the doldrums. In contrast hand-forged silver, however recently produced, has held its value and is sought after by an ever-growing number of informed users. Fundamentally, it is the handworking of precious metals that has captivated people for centuries and still continues to do so.

TABLE SERVICES

The composition of table services affects both quality and condition. The standard service of English flatware tends to be thought of comprising 12 of each of the following:– soup spoons, table knives and forks; dessert knives, forks and spoons; tea or coffee spoons, and a variety of implements for serving. However, many households have had much larger services, to cope with as many as 100 guests! Only a few were made in this great size and the majority of these have been split up over the years. Returning to the realms of more usual silver, many services of a reasonable size have survived and are in use today. Known as canteens when complete with their original wooden fitted cases, a common configuration is that of 36 table knives and forks, 18 or 24 dessert-size knives and forks and 18 spoons. The double number of table-size cutlery was probably intended to accommodate two main courses, one of fish and one of meat. Separate fish knives and forks were introduced around 1840 but only became common towards the end of the 1800s.

Victorian services are the most likely to be found intact, with large plate settings incorporating everything from fruit eaters, sometimes with mother-of-pearl handles, to egg spoons with gilded bowls. To own or to acquire one of these comprehensive services is to have both a sumptuous adornment to any table and an appreciating asset.[1]

TOP
Two silver coffee pots, both produced around 1760. The pot on the left has been later chased during the Victorian era *c.* 1865 with decorations typical of that period.

ABOVE
Pear-shaped tankards. The one of the right is in its original form, the one on the left has been altered completely during the Victorian era. The spout and the unmarked dome cover have been added, the piece has been later chased and the handle has been cut off and ivory heat insulators let in, converting the article into a hot milk jug.

ALTERED PIECES – LEGITIMATE AND FAKE

As already detailed in the previous chapter on styles, fashion has dictated that designs and patterns change periodically, creating a demand for the latest variation in taste. Consequently, silversmiths have often been asked to adapt old-fashioned silver to imitate the new vogue.

OVERCHASING AND RECONSTRUCTION

This practice reached its zenith during the Victorian period, when the preference was for increasingly ornate objects. Very plain items, made between the mid-1700s, and the early 1800s, were overchased with elaborate floral work and foliage, in most cases distorting the fine lines of the originals. Alterations took place because the price of labour meant it was less expensive to change the appearance of an existing item than to commission a new one from scratch. The very nature of sterling silver – its lasting quality – made it a prime candidate for alteration, unlike many of our present-day products with their tendency towards rapid obsolescence. Practically every type of silver item was vulnerable to corruption with later chasing but, fortunately, this procedure was not that widespread.

Another, more insidious form of alteration was to change the function of an article altogether. For example, a tankard could be transformed into a milk jug. This procedure was, and still is, illegal unless the article in question was resubmitted to the nearest assay office so that hallmarks, with new date letters, could be added to indicate the additions. Even today, if re-hallmarking is not arranged, pieces are liable to seizure.

In America, except for a brief period in Baltimore, Maryland, no regulations existed for controlling silver. American manufacturers were not above using psuedo-English hallmarks to lend bogus authenticity to their products. These marks were not even faithful copies of their English counterparts, just crass imitations. The lack of controlled assay marks can make spotting alterations difficult.

In order to identify altered pieces, it is necessary to become familiar with the styles prevalent at different periods. For example, a neo-classical coffee pot (*c.* 1780–90) adorned with chased bulbous flowers and foliage has, almost certainly, been the victim of later decoration.

Recognizing reconstructed pieces is a harder task, but there are some give-away signs. For example on a fruit basket with a missing handle, which would be too costly to replace, the two mounts where the handle would have been originally attached to the border would be clearly visible. This item then might be sold on with a different description, that of a tazza (originally a food-tasting dish, later a dish for bonbons or small delicacies) or a bread basket, for instance. Handles are sometimes taken from trays, kettles separated from their stands, candlesticks parted from their nozzles and cruet frames found minus bottles or central handles. This is usually the result of loss or damage.

On hollow ware silver, look for the rough solder patches that indicate crude joins. Always check that any extras attached by hinge or pinning to the main body of a piece have a matching hallmark.

CUTTING DOWN AND OTHER ALTERATIONS

Flatware has been and is subject to alterations by dealers who want to enhance the value of their goods by changing either the form or the pattern of forks and spoons. The relatively common fiddle pattern can be cut down to the Old English pattern, a rarer and hence more valuable design, thus increasing the value by 30–40 per cent. Engraving a feathered edge or bright cut decoration onto the regular Old English pattern improves the value by 20–30 per cent. This later decoration, however, usually looks too sharp and shiny and is, therefore, quite easy to spot. Originals will have a soft lustre and the decoration have a smoothened appearance. Cut-down fiddle pattern is a little more difficult to confirm. By holding the spoon or the fork by the bowl or prongs with the handle vertical, it can be seen that the shape is not symmetrical, with one side tapering more radically than the other.

Another test to determine whether a piece has been cut-down involves taking the item between the thumb and forefinger, by the edges, and running your finger and thumb along the edge, near the top end (the opposite end to the bowl or prongs). If it feels very sharp, this could signify that it is cut-down fiddle pattern. The die used to produce the design leaves a thinner section than on the equivalent Old English pattern disc.

As a more legitimate alternative to selling on an object as something different, dealers often attempt to make an article more saleable by replacing an absent cruet bottle with a good likeness or matching a spare handle to a cruet frame which is without one. This is perfectly acceptable so long as the vendor selling the altered pieces willingly declares any alterations or substitutions in writing. It can be a costly mistake if you purchase from someone either lacking the expertise to recognize alterations or who pretends not to have sufficient knowledge in this field. (See *Buying and Selling Hints* at the end of this chapter.) Fortunately there are very few pieces that have been drastically altered and most flaws can be easily spotted when examining silverware.

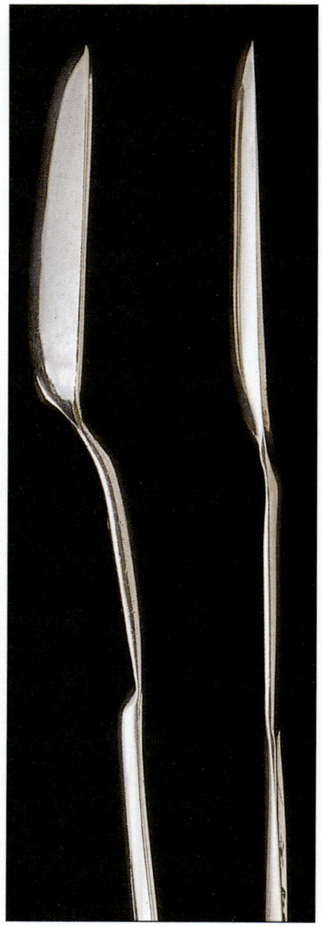

ASSESSING THE WORTH OF ALTERED PIECES

Articles chased long after the date of manufacture are generally thought to be worth the same as other silver items manufactured in the period that the chasing was added, whereas reconstructed articles are probably not worth much more than quarter of the value of the original. Where there are missing parts or later additions, the value is probably a half to two-thirds of the original.

As a general rule, it is not advisable to contemplate purchasing silverware that is not in its original state, unless the price reflects the lower quality. You can ascertain the original value by comparing the defective piece with that of a similar article in perfect condition. Repaired pieces will not improve in value to the same extent as a piece in good order.

Matched tea and coffee sets, as well as cutlery, are quite common, especially the latter. This is when a piece or pieces – usually made by the same silversmith at a different date – has been matched up to an otherwise incomplete set to make it more useful and valuable. Alternatively, quantities of, say, cutlery of the same pattern but by various makers are often grouped together. As long as all the individual pieces are in good condition, this can be an affordable way to acquire sets. Although, it is best to have an original set, these matched sets do appreciate well in value and give the owner a lot of pleasure in their use. If the added patterns on matched sets are noticably varied from that of the originals, the value does diminish by a greater margin.

FAR LEFT

Two silver marrow scoops. The article on the left is in original and fine condition whereas the 'scoop' on the right almost certainly started life as a table spoon and was altered at a later date. Notice the uneven lines and overall form as compared to the article on the left.

LEFT

Side profile of the same two scoops. The article on the left has well-defined and deep bowls, whereas the article on the right is almost shapeless, and where there is curvature it appears distorted.

LEFT

A silver coffee pot produced in 1750, which at some point has lost its original handle (which probably would have been wood) and has been replaced with a silver handle that appears disproportionately large. The handle is not hallmarked and lacks any chased decoration.

FAKES AND DECEPTIONS

Fortunately, the rigid British hallmarking system makes silver harder to fake than any other form of antique. It has always been recognized practice to reproduce earlier items of silverware, with the date and details of the hallmarks always identifying these pieces as faithful copies. However, it is a different matter when reproduction silverware is passed off as an original or made by casting a copy of an object, which includes its real hallmark.

The most common form of silver faking involves taking old hallmarks from either a small, inexpensive item – such as a teaspoon – or from a piece by a prominent maker that is otherwise in poor condition. The hallmark is then let-in to a new or lesser item. This technique can normally be spotted immediately as a line around the hallmarks but, if the faker is particularly skilled, it will be much harder to see. Breathing on the hallmark will expose even the most cunningly hidden solder line. In some instances a whole area containing the hallmark is cut away and replaced. To check for solder lines look inside the piece.

Sometimes cast copies of whole objects have evidence of the old cast hallmark being deleted and new hallmarks applied. This, of course, is legitimate. Cast hallmarks have a stippled effect which can be seen on close examination or with the aid of a magnifying glass. By comparison, an original hallmark will be a clean and smooth stamp.

Different categories of goods tend to follow different configurations of hallmarks, which help to spot fakes. For instance, Victorian coffee and teapots have hallmarks arranged in a square on the base. Marks borrowed from a spoon would be let-in as a straight line. The guide in Chapter 2, Hallmarks, should help to identify how hallmarks should appear. If you look at enough silver you will inevitably come across fakes and, until you are confident at recognizing them, the best advice is to buy only from reputable dealers.

[1]For a fascinating and comprehensive study of flatware see *Silver Flatware, English, Irish and Scottish 1660–1980* by Ian Pickford, pub-lished by The Antique Collectors Club.

BUYING AND SELLING HINTS

The information provided so far in this book will have helped you to become acquainted with many facets of the silver trade, past and present. You should now be able to apply this knowledge to identifying your own pieces and to selecting good pieces from bad when offered for sale. The facts contained below can be most helpful in making an otherwise daunting task a pleasurable experience. Buying silver should always be a pleasure, and selling, of course, should always be as profitable as possible.

BUYING SILVER

The pleasure of buying, owning and using silver can be diminished if the article is unable to fulfil the function intended. Condition is one of the most important factors to take into account when making a purchase, so it is up to the customer to inspect carefully any articles for apparent defects – cracks, leaks, kinks, dents or missing parts.

It is also important to ask the dealer if there are any known weaknesses in the piece. There is no harm in asking him or her, for example, to fill an item with water in the shop to ensure there are no leakages.

Questions of taste and style require personal decisions, but condition affects an object's usefulness and value, as well as your own pleasure in possessing a beautiful, individual piece.

A helpful suggestion when looking at silver with a view to buying is always to carry a hallmark book with you. It will identify whether articles have real hallmarks or whether they are the marks of one of the numerous electroplate makes. Stamps that at a quick glance could be confused with each other, will be clarified by careful inspection with a magnifying glass (see the Bibliography, page 128).

FINDING A REPUTABLE SILVER DEALER

In the UK, it is worth looking for members of LAPADA (The London and Provincial Antique Dealers Association) and BADA (British Antique Dealers Association). Both these bodies demand references and proof of knowledge from joining members; they have sound codes of practice by which members must abide or face expulsion. LAPADA and BADA also act as mediators and arbitrators in difficult circumstances, protecting both customers and traders. Dealers or jewellers who are members normally display the LAPADA and BADA stickers on their doors. The addresses of both bodies are included at the end of this section.

Most large towns in Britain have at least one old-fashioned or family-run jeweller who deals in old and new silver. In America these specialists are found in major cities with a few in small towns. The number of good silver outlets in the States has suffered a decline, as many established firms have been taken over by mass-market jewellery chains, often retaining only the original name. Sadly, silver departments have been allowed to run down or been closed down, since

RIGHT
Silver expert Peter Waldron auctioning a pair of George II wine coolers. The maker's mark is that of Paul de Lamerie overstruck with that of Paul Crespin, 1727.

antique silver and plate do not fit the profile of fast turnover goods. However, a few well-known department stores have long-established silver departments with expert buyers and good stocks.

As a general rule, good jewellery dealers will have a more specialized knowledge than general antiques dealers. Since jewellers have traditionally also been silversmiths, the trading and making of silver articles and jewellery have always been allied. It is advisable to ask if there is an in-house silver expert; in the case of jewellery shops this is normally the owner.

VALUATIONS, APPRAISALS AND RECEIPTS

When purchasing antique silverware, ensure that you receive a receipt from the dealer as proof of purchase. The receipt should give a detailed description of each object, mention any defects and, if the dealer claims that there are none, this should be mentioned as well. If there is any reticence on the part of the dealer to provide this information, it may not be advisable to proceed with the purchase.

If you are purchasing from a source whose knowledge is limited, it is advisable to take your acquisition to an expert. Valuation/appraisal should include details of style and decoration, size and weight, date and make, as well as noting any alteration or additions and, of course, its value. This document can be used for insurance purposes as well as for ascertaining the quality of a piece.

The value stated on the valuation document should be approximately 20-25 per cent greater than the actual value. This will give you adequate cover for 2-3 years, including appreciation and inflation, after which time an updated version should be arranged. If you have a sizeable collection, it is worth calling an appraiser/valuer once a year to hear his/her assessment of market trends.

Other types of valuation that might be useful to obtain are a willing buyer/willing seller valuation – if you are planning to sell goods privately – or a trade price valuation if you wish to sell to a dealer.

Because of risk of theft or damage keep valuations somewhere safe, preferably with a bank, both for insurance claims and to prove that any subsequent damage occurred after the purchase. It is also a good idea to photograph your silverware and to take extra pictures, to record details close-up and hallmarks. Video recordings of your goods *in situ* are also a good tool, and can help the recovery of silver in the event of a robbery. If you do not own a video camera, that is no bar: they are inexpensive to rent and easy to use.

AUCTION HOUSES

Wonderful silverware can be found in auction houses but there are pitfalls which should be avoided.

'Caveat emptor' ('Let the buyer beware') is the general proviso made by both UK and USA auction houses, thus protecting themselves from claims made by purchasers after the event. The major auction houses in London and New York, however, do offer a five-year guarantee.

Because of their limited knowledge, provincial auction houses describe objects in their catalogues by style and date. They are under no obligation to mention any faults, additions or alterations. It is entirely up to the prospective bidder to examine the goods when viewing and recognize any potential problems which could affect the object's value.

On both sides of the Atlantic, licensed auctioneers can sell their own goods alongside those consigned by people, but only in the UK do they have to declare the vendor's identity. The danger of not doing so is that the auctioneer can set a high reserve on his/her own silver, which may include an inflated profit, making these purchases an expensive buy. It is also not unheard of for auctioneers to take bids from the walls, chairs or invisible buyers in an attempt to inflate the final price. In addition, auctioneers are allowed to issue a written disclaimer stating that it is not possible to give a guarantee as to the authenticity of any information supplied about the goods for auction.

Commission is usually payable by both buyer and seller. Rates vary. In most cases, it is based on a percentage of the total bid excluding taxes. The average percentage charge to the seller is 10 per cent. However, sometimes better rates can be negotiated if the items offered are greatly superior in quality, unusual or rare, thereby enhancing the credibility and stature of the auction house. There is usually a reserve price placed on each item, below which the item cannot be sold. If a piece does not reach the reserve price, it is withdrawn or 'brought in', and the seller is usually charged a fee by the auctioneer. Putting goods into an auction without a reserve should only be undertaken if the items in question are of limited value.

Buyers may fare less well with the increase in premium to 15 per cent by the leading auction houses at their more important sales.

Since only the major auction houses offer any protection for buyers, auctions are best left to those in the trade. Buying from expert silver dealers is the safest option. However, if you do wish to try the auction system, consider asking an expert to accompany you to provide advice. He or she will usually charge a fee for this service, but it could save you from making a costly mistake.

PRICES AND HAGGLING

Antique silver and plate have prices with more or less fixed parameters within the trade. These are based on factors described previously. More dramatic fluctuations occur when items are very unusual or of a superior or poor quality.

Like all retailers of luxury goods, silver dealers will probably try to impress you with the fine attributes of a piece; after all, that's their job. Do not be intimidated by the sales patter. Stay calm and avoid making statements that destroy your negotiating position such as "It's the most beautiful thing I have ever seen and I can't live without it". Haggling is a process that most people outside the trade are too embarrassed to try, but with subtlety and tact you can often reduce the purchase price. Suggesting that you only have a certain amount of money to spend and that the article in question exceeds the limit you have set for the purchase may encourage the dealer to make concessions. The important thing is not to be either meek or aggressive when discussing the price.

If the piece in question is of a superior quality or very rare there will probably be little or no movement on price but, as most pieces are not in this category, haggling is always worth a try. Defects and poor condition are other reasons for bargaining, though it generally is not recommended that items with defects are purchased.

Some dealers have a policy of fixed prices, claiming that their goods have been priced at a reasonable level in the first instance.

Attempting to lower the price in department stores is worth considering, as often a sale is helpful to the turnover of a silver department wishing to meet monthly sales targets, especially as mark-ups are likely to be high. Always ask to speak to the department manager, as he or she is likely to be the only person with the authority to give discounts.

The ultimate price paid by the customer for silverware is often a subjective decision. The commitment to buy an article of silver can be based on emotional as well as on investment values. When all is said and done you will probably pay what the object is personally worth to you. If you are worried that your heart is influencing your head too much, try asking the dealer what he/she would pay for the article if it was returned for resale in two year's time. The amount quoted, allowing for tax, is also a good indication of the dealer's profit margin. To explain, dealers are always going to sell silver at its market value, however little an item cost them. Although values fluctuate, it can be assumed that values appreciate at roughly 10 per cent per annum. If the dealer is asking, for example, $1,500 today and is prepared to offer $1,200 in two years' time it is likely therefore that the piece has a present trade value of $1,000. So he or she has added on in this case, two years' appreciation to the original cost, plus his $300 mark-up for profit, to reach $1,500.

Many department stores double their original purchase cost as do some dealers and high-street jewellers. Specialist silver dealers and some antique dealers, particularly in the UK, work on much lower margins and are therefore unable or unwilling to offer large discounts.

A final note about buying silver. If you choose the finest quality you cannot go far wrong. Condition is everything and people will always be prepared to pay for the best.

SELLING SILVER

The same sources (apart from department stores) and guidelines can be used for selling silver as for buying. The exceptions are auction houses, which will be covered in this section.

To ascertain the value of an object, it is advisable to obtain comparative price indications. Reputable auctioneers can suggest an estimated price that the silver might fetch at auction and a reserve price under which any items will not be sold. The reserve price will be close to rock bottom while the estimated price is usually on the high side. However, it must be borne in mind that, occasionally, prices higher than the estimated price are achieved. Comparing these two prices will give some idea of the trade value. Articles can also be taken to appraisers or dealers for their opinion. All parties may charge a fee, the basis or amount of which should be established in the first instance.

Once you have an idea of the trade value you have three options:

1 To sell to a dealer or jeweller (department stores are not geared up to buy from individuals). Goods can be offered at a price a little higher than auction price since the dealer will not be paying auctioneer's commission (see 2 below).

The advantage of selling to a trade buyer is that no advertising is involved and that payment is instant. Bear in mind that a dealer buys to sell again and must therefore make a profit on the transaction.

2 To sell by auction. But be aware that both you and the buyer will have to pay the auctioneer's commission in most cases (usually 10–12 per cent for each party). In addition, many months may elapse between submitting items for auction, the date on which they are actually sold and, again, when payment is settled.

3 If you don't have an interested friend or relative, try advertising in a trade journal using a PO Box number (for security reasons). Meet any interested parties at the bank or safe deposit building and take payment only by certified cheque, banker's order or cash. Alternatively wait for any cheque to be cleared before handing over your silver.

When selling to other members of the public, friends or relatives, you are entitled to ask more than could be realized from a dealer or auction house. A suggested amont is 30–50 per cent more than the auction estimate; this will usually be less than the retail price at many places and so fair to both parties. Don't be surprised if they wish to haggle over the price – it works both ways!

Antique Appraisers Association of America
60 East 42nd Street
New York, NY

British Antique Dealers Association (BADA)
20 Rutland Gate
London SW7

London and Provincial Antique Dealers Association (LAPADA)
Suite 214
535 King's Road
London SW10

Styles – 1700 – 1930

ABOVE

Charles I pilgrim bottle (wine bottle) London, 1663. 15½″ high.

Changes of styles are dictated by many different factors – affluence, the need for austerity, social customs, fashion and foreign influences. Silver styles were also subject to the changes of architectural and interior design as well as the silver manufacturing and decorative techniques prevalent at the time. As frequently happens now, past designs came back into fashion for example neo-classical forms were repeated by the Edwardians. With a few minor deviations, American silver styles generally followed the English patterns.

The style of a piece alone cannot tell us when a piece was made: other factors must be taken into consideration, such as knowledge of social history and hallmarks. Although we have sought to illustrate pieces typical of the period, silver was often created on commission, which did not necessarily reflect the fashions of that particular era. For example, in dating the pilgrim bottle shown here, the masks and chased ornamentation in the form of acanthus leaves reappeared in 1760, the early 1800s and the Victorian era. To our knowledge this type of vessel was not common after the 17th century. This information, combined with an examination of the marks, enables us to date the piece.

RIGHT

Pair of Queen Anne silver gilt table candlesticks and snuffer stand, fitted with scissor-type snuffer. Candlesticks and stand made by Edward Ironside of London in 1702. The simplicity of line is synonymous with this era. The sunken bell-shaped bases and balluster columns are aesthetically pleasing.

BRITAIN, THE FIRST 130 YEARS: 1700–1830

The styles of eighteenth- and early nineteenth-century silverware have distinctive characteristics – readily identifiable, once one is familiar with their features. Thereafter designs tended to be more eclectic in nature. Queen Anne (1702–1714) gave her name to the plain designs that were in vogue before and after her reign while the Georgian period – lasting from 1714 to 1830 – reflected a whole range of styles.

Eighteenth-century English silverware falls into three main periods – Queen Anne, rococo and Adam (classic).

QUEEN ANNE

As previously discussed, the higher Britannia standard of silver was still the legal requirement until 1720. The greater silver content of this standard forced silversmiths to concentrate on plain, simple body shapes and decoration. This was because alloy was softer and more prone to wear than sterling silver.

ABOVE

George I silver jug and shaving basin by premier silversmith Simon Pantin, London, 1717. Jug 7½" high, basin 13½" in length.

LEFT

Charles II parcel gilt cagework cup and cover *c.* 1670, 8" high. The rich adornment was in complete contrast to its predecessors of the Puritan period. The decorations are executed in a cruder fashion than those in later periods.

Plain and pierced cut-card work, flutings, punch leaf outlines and on the larger pieces cast shells, masks, animal and human figures were the uncluttered decorative forms employed. The pleasing proportions, balance and simplicity of such pieces have ensured their popularity ever since.

Although these plain forms were austere and silver displays more fashionably restrained than in the flamboyant times of Charles II, sparing expense was not a consideration. Newly rich merchants, prospering from the demand for exotic imports from the Colonies, sought to improve their domestic arrangements. Large houses boasted substantial silver wine fountains and cisterns; ladies possessed toilet sets of 30 plus pieces. The skill of the silversmiths and the quality of goods were better during this period than at any other time.

Innovative everyday items of silverware were made for the first time during the reign of Queen Anne. Soup tureens, sauce boats and cruet frames were new additions to the dining-room. Teapots, coffee pots, cream jugs and casters were introduced as tea, coffee and chocolate increased in popularity. These and other items were ogee-bodied or pear-shaped. The Queen was a great patron of horse-racing and the sport flourished thanks to her interest, resulting in manufacture of many a two-handled racing cup! Snuff-taking was also fashionable so silver snuff boxes became the ideal containers.

Of the early makers, David Willaume, Pierre Platel, Simon Pantin, Pierre Harache and William Fawdery best exemplified the finest work of the period.

ABOVE

George I panelled octagonal silver teapot attributed to Edmund Pearce, London, 1722 and panelled coffee pot, Britannia standard silver, London, 1722.

LEFT

George I side handled silver chocolate pot, by David Tangueray. The side handle was very popular during the Queen Anne and George I period. The animal head opening, strap work around the spout and general form could also be found in France in the same period. Chocolate was the most popular drink at this time, and the various chocolate houses were social venues.

ROCOCO

Rococo style, the last phase of baroque, was French in origin. Its rise to fame was due to the influence of the Huguenot immigrants who settled throughout the British Isles. The name, derived from the French *rocaille*, meaning rock or shell-like, and its inspiration from natural Chinese and Gothic forms.

The 200 or so Huguenot silversmiths who fled to England from France in 1685, following the Revocation of the Edict of Nantes, were responsible for some of the most elaborate pieces of the first half of the century. Their work was executed in a heavier gauge of metal to an acknowledged high standard. English silversmiths were jealous of the Huguenots' ability to obtain commissions using the latest French styles and much acrimony resulted. Many eminent English smiths responded to the competition by adopting the fashionable Louis XIV styles, at the same time continuing to favour the plainer designs. The latter were highly popular until around 1725 and were still preferred by some well into the middle of the century. The reintroduction of the old metal standard led ornate decoration to be fashionable again and for the next 40 years the highly chased French style was dominant.

Across the decorative arts forms, the rococo style was light and airy, often asymmetrical and abstract in form. Rococo silverware was no exception. Marine motifs, floral sprays, ribbons, shells, symbolic figures and animal heads were some of the decorative forms chased, embossed, cast or applied to silver objects. The shell was the most common decoration and was often incorporated with scrolls on to the borders of trays and dishes.

ABOVE

This silver inkstand made by John Luff, London, 1738, has fine lines. Although this shows scroll and shell ornamentation, it is still quite simple and it bridges the gap between the two periods.

The most famous and prolific English maker of rococo silverware was Paul de Lamerie, a Huguenot whose early work was in the Queen Anne style. Although native English silver-smiths had to follow the fashion, their work not as ornate as their successful Huguenot counterparts, de Lamarie, Blanchard, Harache, Courtauld and a host of others. De Lamerie is not only considered one of the finest exponents of rococo, but one of the finest silversmiths of all time.

During the reign of George II, the demand for household silver enjoyed a far greater boom than in the first quarter of the century. Serving dishes, tureens, salt-cellars and the like were now used in more modest homes. The volume of tea imported increased dramatically, cutting its cost and making it available to a wider audience. Tea gardens and coffee houses were firmly established and widely patronized. A large number of rococo tea caddies, sugar bowls, cream jugs and teapots still exist to prove the growing importance of this beverage. Large and elaborate epergnes and centrepieces were imported from France to grace Georgian dining room tables.

The fashion for rococo reached its height by the 1750s. Simultaneously, Gothic, rustic and Chinese styles also attracted designers and makers, enjoying a brief success. Open-work, mirroring fret-work on Chippendale's elegant furniture, was also in vogue.

RIGHT

George I silver sugar caster (left) by Samuel Wood, London, 1745, a silver gilt coffee pot by Thomas Whipham, London, 1754, and a tea caddy by Christian Hillan, 1741. All show the popular rococo style with stirling scrolls and foliage. Note the ebonized wood handle is a later replacement.

LEFT

A George II tea kettle on lampstand made by Thomas Farren, London, 1742. Note the cast openwork aprons between the supports, the stylized shell mounts and mermen handle decorations. These and other naturalistic forms of embellishment reached their zenith during the rococo era. The woven wicker covering was used as a heat insulator.

BELOW

A set of two tea caddies and sugar box by Paul de Lamerie, premier silversmith, London, 1738. The decorations have been executed to the highest standards. These are lockable caddies, because tea was a fairly rare and expensive commodity at the time.

RIGHT

A pair of George II table candlesticks, in the Chinoiserie taste, made by Philips Garden, London, 1756. Chinese coolies are supporting the vaguely pagoda-style stems, combined with the rococo scrollwork and shell motif. 12½" high.

ADAM OR CLASSIC PERIOD

The switch from rococo to classical influences was the most extreme change of style in the century. It was inspired by revived interest in Greco-Roman art, and closely allied different decorative art forms.

During the mid-1700s, the excavation, first of Herculaneum and later Pompeii, revealed many beautiful bronze and silver objects preserved by the volcanic ash and lava which had engulfed both cities when Vesuvius erupted in AD 79. The published drawings of the finds showed classical forms that begged to be copied and adapted by silversmiths. French and other continental smiths were the first to produce goods based on these ancient designs which made a refreshing change from the extravagant grandeur of rococo. By 1765, English smiths had followed suit.

In England, the architect Robert Adam – who spent several years studying ancient architecture in Italy – and his brother James, were busy designing buildings in the new neo-classical style. Robert Adam also used his considerable abilities to design furniture and other decorative accoutrements to complement his classical houses and mansions. Recorded drawings show that Adam was specifically commissioned to produce silverware designs for wealthy patrons, which were then realized by silversmiths. He is also known to have published drawings which were modified by silversmiths and subjected to their own interpretations, to better suit the average household.

RIGHT

A pair of silver vegetable dishes and covers made by Thomas Heming, London, 1767. 5½" high. The simpler cleaner style became fashionable again at this time. This is reminiscent of Queen Anne in its panelled form, but has finer, more delicate lines, the hallmark of the Adam period. The rococo-style highly ornamented pineapple finial is mixed with the simpler Adam lines.

BELOW

A set of four fine quality cast silver table candlesticks made by John Carter, London, 1774, 19¾" high. Bellflower swags, fine beaded borders and mounts, and acanthus leaves are typical of the Adam classical decorative style.

LEFT

A set of four silver table candlesticks made in Sheffield in 1775 with the maker's mark overstruck by that of John Carter of London. These candlesticks, of stamped construction and a relatively thin gauge of metal, have been filled with tar to give them both strength and weight. Often, steel rods were also inserted to give them additional weight and stability. These are some of the earliest examples of the new industrialization taking place in England.

ABOVE

A silver George III teapot and stand, London, 1798, with overstruck maker's mark Wakelin and Garrard.

The Adam style favoured ovoid outlines and Greek or Roman vase shapes. Decoration followed classical themes – floral swags, laurel leaves, knotted ribbons, ram and lion heads, masks and figures. Beaded mouldings, pierced work on trays, entrée dishes and baskets were prevalent. Candlesticks in the form of fluted columns topped by capitals became widespread.

The development of fused plate and, the advent of steam which made milling, rolling and stamping sheet possible, greatly increased the volume and availability of silverware. As previously noted, Mathew Boulton was the finest producer of fused plate silverware. On the subject of mechanization, the pottery manufacturer, Josiah Wedgwood, greatly impressed silversmiths with his ability to produce by mechanical means accurate, high-quality designs in the classical mode. More silver of this period was made for household use rather than display purposes. New items made available included Argyles (covered sauce tureens), entrée dishes with hot water compartments and tea urns.

In addition to Mathew Boulton, other pre-eminent exponents of the neo-classical revival in England included Frederick Kandler, Hester Bateman, Robert Hennell and John Carter. Paul Revere, the son of an immigrant Huguenot silversmith, produced outstanding work in America.

The economic restraints of the 1790s meant a short phase of plain and sparsely decorated silverware, and the Adam style went into a decline.

LEFT

A set of three dessert baskets on stands by John Wakelin and William Taylor, London 1789/90. The Adam style designs abound on these articles – note the cast ram's head ring holders, the stylized wave pattern borders, ribbons and medallions, as well as the overall geometric symmetry.

LEFT

A substantial silver soup tureen and cover fitted with a removable liner made by Robert Sharp, London, 1794. The more massive appearance of this piece shows the transition of the period, and the beading, medallions and bellflower swags with ribbons will give way to the more solid fluting and the heavier gadroon borders. This transitional period was dominated by the influence of Paul Storr who was to become the greatest silversmith of the 19th century.

ABOVE

A silver epergne by Robert Hennell of London, 1778, one of the premier makers. This centrepiece not only typifies the style of the era, but also illustrates the necessity to use the minimum amount of silver at a time when the metal was very costly and the duty payable on silver articles was high.

EMPIRE DESIGNS AND REGENCY SILVER

The modest goods of the last decade of the 18th century were eventually superseded at the beginning of this century by two parallel styles: Empire, popular in France since the 1780s and favoured by Napoleon, and Regency, the English equivalent. Again, these styles borrowed from the ancient Greek and Roman civilizations as well as reaching further back in time to stylized Egyptian images. Both furniture and silver benefited from the Egyptian revival, stimulated by Napoleon's activities in that country.

Ornamentation included lyres, lotus blossoms, winged busts, horns of plenty, lion's feet, garlands, fluting, beaded borders, human heads, faces and leaves. Heroic themes were favoured, as were masive forms and heavy gilding.

Silversmiths of this period often had problems translating designs from the pens of highly imaginative artists. Most of the designers' drawings for Empire pieces were based on originals in bronze, stone or clay, often quite unsuited to silver.

In the early 1800s English silversmiths faithfully copied French styles, but the resultant silverware was considered too formal for English tastes. Soon the English interpretation of the style, Regency silver, evolved. Prominent English craftsmen such as Paul Storr, Benjamin Smith and Digby Scott – who worked for the Royal Goldsmiths, Rundell, Bridge and Rundell – made a considerable contribution to the development of the Regency style.

TOP

A pair of silver tureens and covers and a pair of entrée dishes and covers made by Paul Storr, London, 1800. Note the clean lines and the gadroon borders.

ABOVE

These four cast candlesticks with their trumpet-shaped columns and gadroon borders typify the early 1800s. This set was made in London in 1801 by Richard Cooke.

LEFT

A pair of silver wine coolers made by Benjamin Smith for the firm of Rundell Bridge and Rundell, London, 1807. The entwined serpents forming the handles and the egg and dart borders exemplify this period.

ABOVE LEFT

A pair of George III silver wine coolers, made by Storr and Co, London, 1817. The multifacetted bodies are highly unusual, but the leaf, shell and gadroon borders, and the acorn and oak leaf clusters are typical of the years 1810–1820.

ABOVE

Silver tea urn by Benjamin & James Smith with a finial made by Paul Storr, London, 1810.

LEFT

A three-light and five-light silver gilt candelabra by Rundell, Bridge and Rundell, London, *c.* 1815. The incorporation and revival of the acanthus leaves and the introduction of the Egyptian motifs signify changing tastes.

ONE HUNDRED YEARS OF VARIETY: 1830–1930

The death of George IV in 1830 signified both the end of the Regency period and the last days of serious artistic patronage. This caused a serious decline in the standard of design. In addition, while the uniform precision of the machine made mass-production possible it also was replacing the individual design and characteristics of handmade articles by skilled smiths. By 1840 electroplating had become a key element in the triumph of mass production, its cost-effective products using a minimal amount of silver. However, many craftsmen stood aside from the path of so-called progress, and continued to make exemplary silverware.

From 1830 to the turn of the century, through the reigns of William IV and Queen Victoria, designs were many and various, borrowing from a wide range of historical sources. More firms followed in the footsteps of Rundell, Bridge and Rundell by employing in-house designers.

ABOVE

William IV silver gilt inkstand, made by Benjamin Smith, London, 1835. Note the bulbous melon-shaped pots, a design that recurs throughout this period. The scalloped and panelled body and domed ink-well covers have a stylized shell motif. This, allied with the floral finials and scrolling supports, is a departure in style from the massive designs of the early 1800s.

A POT-POURRI OF STYLES

The rococo revival started in the reign of George IV and continued through that of William IV. It combined elements of French rococo with the outlines of Regency style. Vessels were generally lower and broader than earlier and heavily hand-embossed, a characteristic that was to continue in fashion until the 1860s.

Naturalistic shapes burgeoned during the 1820s, reaching their peak in 1840, though they were still being sold in the late 19th century. First handles, spouts and other applied items borrowed their designs from plants and leaves, then whole pieces began to resemble plants or even trees dipped in silver. Examples include silver vessels that might be shaped as large

ABOVE

Set of four William IV silver dishes and covers, each surmounted by an elaborate cast finial with game motif made by Storr and Mortimer of London *c.* 1830. Two are shown with Sheffield Plate bases with hot water jackets. In the foreground is a suite of open salts by Hunt and Roskell, London *c.* 1850. The finely cast animals were particularly popular from 1830 onwards, as new worlds were explored and discovered throughout the Empire.

LEFT

William IV silver tea kettle on lampstand with burner, made by Paul Storr, London, 1836. The bulbous melon pattern body is a distinguishing feature of the era.

LEFT

A Victorian silver gilt sweetmeat bowl and cover, made by R & S Garrard and Co, London, 1839, 9¼" high. Again, the representations of animals denote the Victorian period, although it draws from the rococo period with the naturalistic floral and foliage work.

BELOW

A shaped oval soup tureen and cover by Reily and Stover, London, 1838. Note again the bulbous melon body.

flower blossoms and centrepieces made as trees with leaf-like dishes.

A backlash against the effects of industrialization on the decorative arts saw a large-scale revival of the Gothic style, seen as a return to traditional techniques. A few silver pieces in the style were made. Though some were produced for domestic purposes such designs were more suitable and therefore more popular for ecclesiastical silver. A W N Pugin was the style's leading light. Revived Renaissance style enjoyed a spell of popularity from the 1840s, thanks to a handful of French designers, one of whom, Antoine Vechte, was encouraged to settle in England.

By the mid-1860s the classical style was back in vogue, as seen at the great industrial exhibitions of 1862 and 1871. New textural variations were achieved by matting and burnishing areas, and flat-chasing or engraving was preferred to the embossed decorations of the previous century.

ABOVE

A parcel gilt cup, flanked by a pair of parcel gilt standing salts, by R & S Garrard and Co, London, 1855. Exquisite detailed casting and a variety of different influences incorporating Byzantium and Gothic. The satin finish background is also typical of the Victorian period and the bulbous lobes and fluting signify designs and techniques allied to the era.

RIGHT

An electroplated parcel gilt sideboard dish by Elkington & Co. *c.* 1875, diameter 21¼". Constructed using the electrotype process.

BELOW LEFT

A pair of fine quality sterling silver wine coolers, illustrating the rococo revival with their stylized wavy rims. The encrusted vine shell-like pattern mounts combined with the above-mentioned decorations suggest revival rather than original. These coolers were made in London by Benjamin Smith, in 1840 for presentation to Sir Thomas Philips for his heroic defence against the Chartist rioters.

RIGHT

Sterling silver cruet frame with cut glass bottles, some surmounted by domed silver covers. There is a distinctly Indian feel shown in both the form and the style of engraving. Made in 1879, London, by Barnard Bros.

ABOVE

Victorian hand-engraved silver-plated teapot. Its pagoda form gives it an Oriental feel although the decorations are strictly English. Made in Sheffield by Atkin Brothers *c.* 1870.

LIBERTY AND THE GUILD OF HANDICRAFT

A passion for all things Japanese developed when Japan started to trade with the outside world in the late 1870s. Japanese-style silverware, introduced to the public by Liberty & Co, was decorated with birds, fans, bamboo, cherry blossom and other oriental motifs. Liberty & Co was founded in 1875 by Arthur Lasenby Liberty, a friend of William Morris. The company was influential in popularizing the art nouveau style. Its first silver range was inspired by Celtic motifs.

Freelance designer Christopher Dresser (1834–1904) was the first English person to produce radically new forms for silver manufacturers. His simple, plain creations were ahead of their time and would have been in harmony with the streamline designs of the 1920s and 1930s. William Morris's Arts and Craft Movement, inspired by the writings of John Ruskin, spawned the Guild and School of Handicraft. Founded by Charles Robert Ashbee in the 1880s, it aimed to hand-produce fine metal, wood and leather goods. The Guild, which became particularly renowned for its hammered and enamelled silverware, and aimed to make a reasonably priced hand-wrought plate. By the mid-1890s the Guild's trademark style of flowing, curved lines had evolved into a variant of art-nouveau, which was rapidly spreading throughout Europe. Intertwined motifs, exaggerated loop handles and use of enamel and semi-precious stones and visible hammermarks were notable features of the Guild's style.

The Guild's influence was widespread, and this in fact was partly its downfall, as larger manufacturers such as Messrs Hutton of Sheffield and Liberty & Co, competed, emulating the Guild style with their own hand-finished, die-stamped items. Regrettably, the Guild was forced to close in 1909, although its ideals were carried into the 20th century by a new generation of individual craftsmen.

FAR LEFT

A large Victorian hand-engraved silver goblet made by John Aldwinkle and James Slater, London, 1881 showing the oriental influence prevalent around the late 1870s and early 1880s.

LEFT

An important sterling silver and enamel vase by Liberty & Co, designed by Archibald Knox, set with six pale green cabochons, Birmingham 1900. Whilst this is a particulaly important example of Knox's designs for Liberty & Co, it typifies in a single piece the source of much of his inspiration. Having roots in the Isle of Man, Knox himself was both impressed and influenced by the purity and simplicity of Celtic design, as is so clearly illustrated here. He also employs the revolutionary concept of decorating a piece with stones of virtually no intrinsic value, of interest for their inherent form and colour.

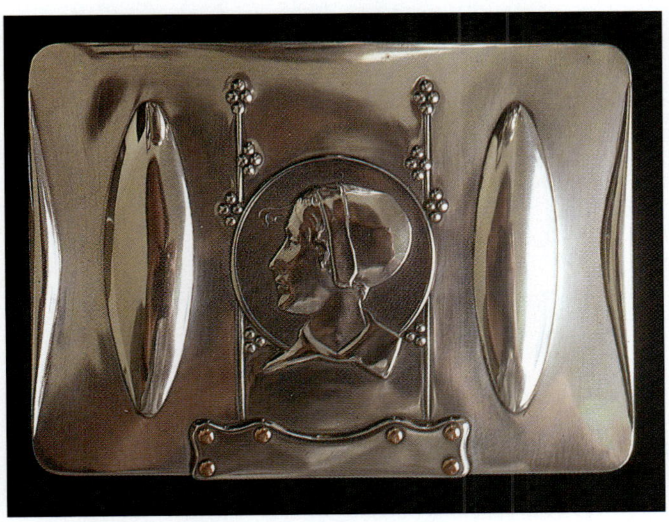

LEFT

Cover of an Arts and Crafts jewel casket with gilded rivet decoration on the hinge. Made by W C Connel, 1899.

ABOVE

The clean lines of this triangular wine jug typify the Arts and Crafts period. This piece was produced in 1909 by Hukin & Heath of Birmingham.

RIGHT

Egyptian Revival sterling silver-gilt dessert service with four servers and sugar sifter in fitted case, Elkington & Co, 1885. An excellent example of the exotic allure the pharaohs held for the recently 'liberated' British public. Until the Great Exhibition of 1851 British silver and its design rested firmly in the past. This exhibition was a watershed not only for British design but also for the British public's acceptance of the new, unusual and exotic.

BELOW

A Victorian silver tea and coffee set made by W R Smiley, London, 1853. The panelled lids and spreading bases combined with panels of foliage and floral work give the overall signs of Victoriana.

ABOVE

Three Victorian cast silver candelabra in the rococo revivalist style. Made by R & S Garrard, London, weight 624 troy ounces!

LEFT

The beloved silver-plated biscuit barrel in all its glory. Hand-chased with florid decorations set against a mottled ground, and interspersed with circular medallions. Although mostly produced in Britain during the middle and latter part of the Victorian era, it was, and is, a most popular article on both sides of the Atlantic. Some were made in sterling silver, but the vast majority were made in silver plate, as was this, *c.* 1865. It is undoubtedly true that there are far more biscuit barrels in America than there are in their country of origin.

ABOVE

Sterling silver tea and coffee set depicting the signs of the zodiac surrounded by geometric patterns and swirling foliage. The form and decoration illustrate the influence of Indian designs on Victorian life. Made by Hamilton and Inches, Edinburgh, 1872.

ABOVE

This silver tea and coffee set made by Barnard Bros. but retailed by Elkington in 1874, is unusual in that it was an experiment in design that did not become popular for another 30 years.

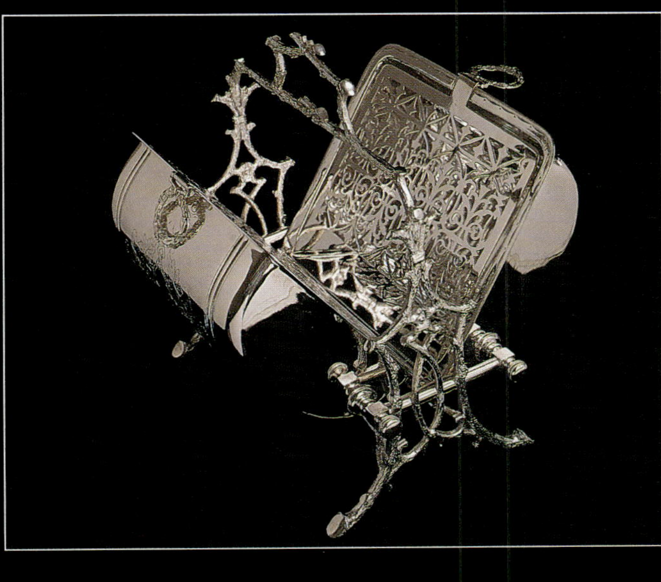

LEFT

A hinged and folding biscuit box made in Sheffield around 1880. This article has the typical stylized bark framework. The interior grills slot neatly into the centre after the biscuit box has been fully opened. These pieces were often used for nuts, berries, sweets and candy etc.

ABOVE

This silver-plated dinner gong, *c.* 1880, with its cast stylized bark frame, was most popular during the Victorian period.

LEFT

A silver tea and coffee set of can shaped form made by John Mappin, Sheffield, 1877. The bodies and covers are hand engraved with a fern and leaf pattern. Interiors of the cream jug and sugar bowl are gilded. Tea and coffee sets in the can form are only found from the late 1870s through to the early 1900s

LEFT

Another popular item from the Victorian era was the egg coddler. The interior is fitted with a removable frame to hold four eggs. Boiling water was poured in and the burner beneath set alight. This was then brought to the table and seven minutes later the eggs were ready. Sheffield, *c.* 1880.

LEFT

A silver gilt fruit serving bowl with matching spoon, by John Newton Mappin, London, 1892. The Egyptian motif can be seen clearly on the spoon although the bowl itself does not exhibit the Egyptian influence. The fanned shell (scallop) decorations as well as the scrolling and foliage indicate a rococo influence.

LEFT

A lady's travelling dresser set in its original fitted case, made by William Comyns, 1894. This rococo-style set contains silver boxes and jars. Many travelling dresser sets made both before and after this one incorporate glass jars with silver covers, as well as such necessary items as writing pads and implements and/ or sewing kits and manicure sets.

ABOVE

This sumptuous claret jug with its highly ornamented rock crystal body and silver gilt mounts was made during the latter part of Queen Victoria's reign. The opulent style draws upon a variety of origins: Middle Eastern, oriental and European. Made by Walter & Charles Sissons, Sheffield, 1909.

LIBERTY AND THE GUILD OF HANDICRAFT

RIGHT

Tobacco casket in sterling silver and enamel, Omar Ramsden & Alwyn C E Carr, handmade and fully inscribed with the unusually full signature 'Omar Ramsden & Alwyn C. E. Carr Made Me 1902'. The assymetric interlocking circle and enamel design on the lid and the flower and water motif on the side make this very English art nouveau box far more appealing than the more bombastic architectural styles normally associated with the maker. Once again this piece shows how a strong oriental influence can manifest itself on a totally traditional Western form. The shape of this footed box has been in existence in Western decorative arts and furniture since at least the 17th century. With the vertical decoration of lilies emerging through rippling water it is as typically Japanese as one could find. The lid itself goes one stage beyond this and abstracts the concept of water to a degree normally only found in the most subtle of Japanese scroll paintings.

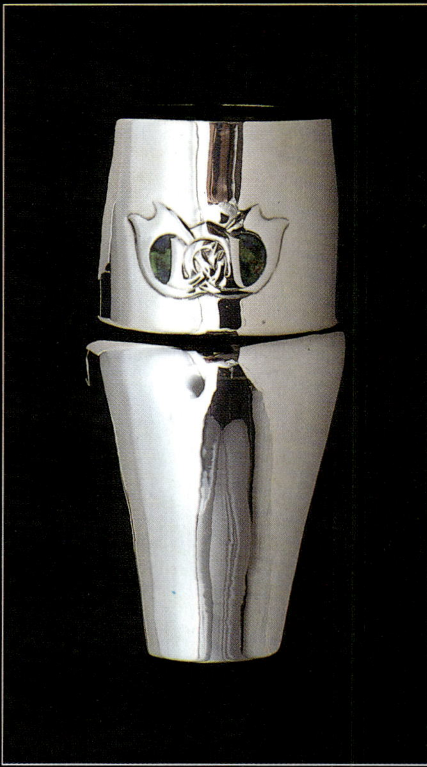

ABOVE

Sterling silver box with enamel 'thistle and spade' decoration, Liberty & Co, Birmingham 1899. This is a typical example of English naturalism of the kind so popular with the then prolific and flourishing Guild of Handicraft workshops. Despite being fully hallmarked by Liberty & Co, the decoration almost has the hand of the great doyen of the Guild – C R Ashbee – about it. Although as yet there is no known proof of any collaboration in existence, this is still a field in which new information is constantly being unearthed.

LEFT

Sterling silver and enamel 'Cymric' vase, Liberty & Co, Birmingham, 1903. This vase shows another interpretation of Celtic knot design with enamel used purely to highlight the form. The fact that the enamel creates the impression of an almost abstract owl's head is not accidental: one of the most fundamental aspects of Celtic design was organic delineation of the elements of nature in everyday life.

RIGHT

Sterling silver coaster with enamel decoration in the form of bats on each handle, Liberty & Co, Birmingham 1906. As with the 'Cymric' vase the bat form is distilled to its simplest essence, and is only clearly apparent when viewed from above.

ABOVE

Sterling silver and three-colour gilt Aesthetic teapot with fugu fish finial, fully hallmarked for Frederick Elkington, Elkington & Co, London 1880. This piece clearly demonstrates Elkington's mastery of combining East with West, for while it is a sublime example of orientalist decoration, the teapot itself remains steadfastly British.

ART NOUVEAU AND ART DECO

The passion for the flowing, intertwining lines of art nouveau swept across Europe from the 1880s and lasted until the beginning of the First World War in 1914. It was widely adopted for graphic design, fabrics, jewellery and architectural metalwork, and in building design. Unlike earlier fashions, art nouveau only affected a small part of the total silver output of the period; it was not suited to mass manufacture.

During these years the importance of artist-craftsmen (as opposed to those who just assembled stamped parts) diminished as hand-crafted silver became the exception rather than the rule. Except for the work of those who followed William Morris, few new designs were initiated.

Gilbert Marks, Omar Ramsden and Alwyn Carr, some of the new generation of individual craftsmen, carried on the ideals and traditions of the Guild and School of Handicraft. Other notable designers and craftsmen of the 20th century include Harold Stabler (also known for his work for London Transport), Leslie Durbin, Cyril Shiner and R G Baxendale, Charles Rennie Mackintosh, H G Murphy and A Edward Jones. Many of them were encouraged by The Worshipful Company of Goldsmiths, who organized design competitions and had a presence at exhibitions both at home and abroad. The fact that the survivors succeeded was due to the originality of their designs and the quality of their work.

Mass-made silverware lacked aesthetic beauty and any spark of creativity, constantly copying the older styles. The social base of the buying public had also grown, particularly after the First World War. The new clients were interested in buying replicas from the past rather in in the work of contemporary designers. The factories, knowing that the tooling investment required to produce new patterns and forms was disproportionate to potential sales, were happy to repeat classical patterns again and again.

Art deco, fashionable from 1920 until 1940, followed on from art nouveau. Its simple use of squares, circles and triangles suited the post-war mood and found favour with a public who was keen to distance itself from the elaborate designs of Edwardian and Victorian England. The style was readily adopted throughout the decorative disciplines by Lalique, Chanel and Schiaparelli amongst others. Silver designs were elegant and stylish. The most popular items, such as cigarette cases, cocktail shakers and powder compacts had the glamourous associations required by consumers, wishing to shake off the horror of the war. The angular lines of the Jazz Age style were particularly well served by the glinting, luminescent quality of silver.

ABOVE LEFT

This sterling silver vase with its swirling cast and applied handles is a forerunner to the even more stylized forms of the art nouveau period. Made in London, 1905.

LEFT

An art nouveau-style silver vase, with stylized elongated handles and multi-facetted body. London, 1902.

RIGHT

With the advent of photography, the necessity for photo frames became apparent. The frame on the left is by William Hair Haster, Birmingham, 1915. The frame on the right is made by Arthur & John Zimmerman, Birmingham, 1916.

LEFT

Sterling silver three-handled cup with lion decoration on foot, Ramsden & Carr, 1905. This cup illustrates a strong feel for medievalism right down to the applied decoration of heraldic lions, with the sinuous form that we have come to associate with art nouveau, incorporated within the 'flying buttress' handles.

ABOVE

This inkstand was photographed to best illustrate the overall design. The art nouveau pattern is hand-chased onto the silver base, the two compressed ball green ink-wells are each surmounted by hinged circular silver covers with open work flattened mounts. Made by William Hutton, London, 1901.

RIGHT

Sterling silver fruit bowl and two side dishes made by Hukin & Heath, Birmingham, 1923. The combination of ivory and silver was very popular during the 1930s, and reflected in the ivory handles.

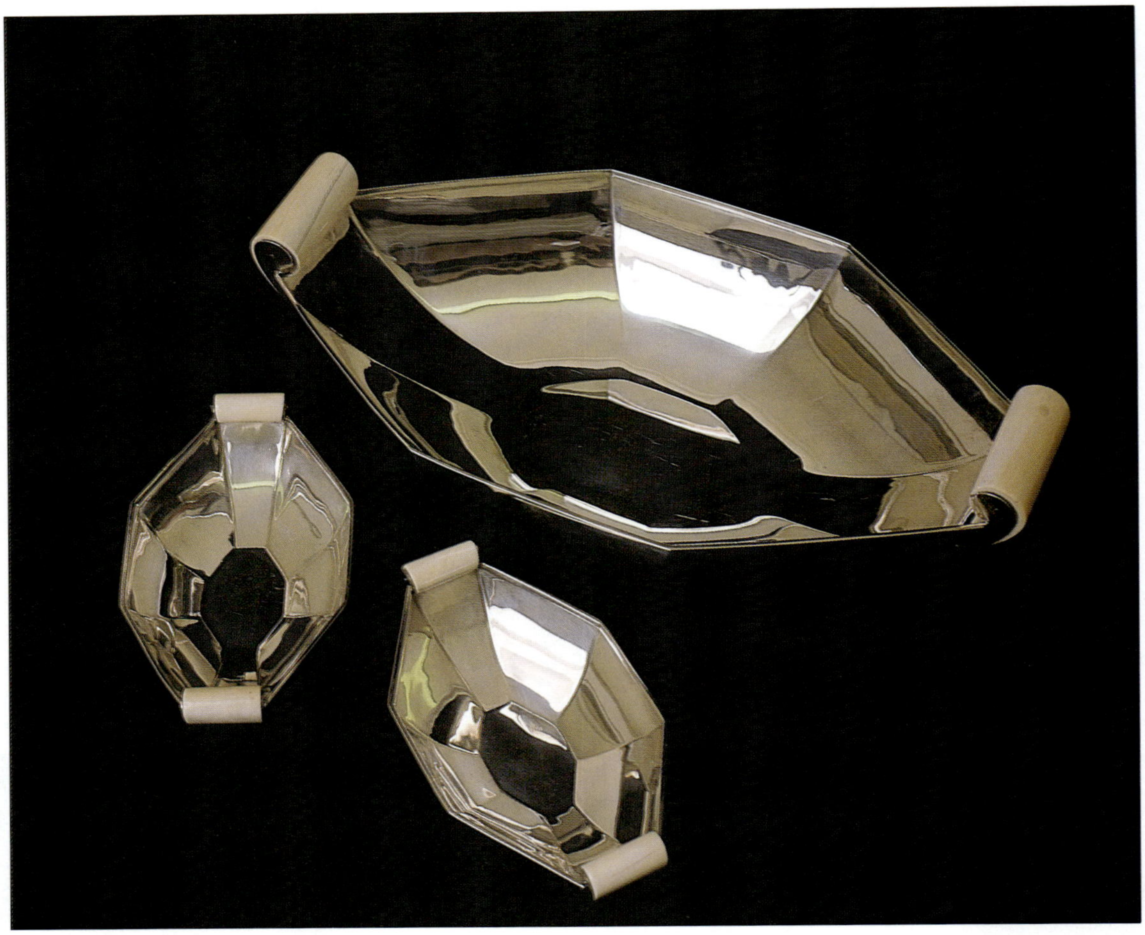

BELOW

A sterling silver panelled tea and coffee service with fruitwood handles and finials made in Birmingham, 1940. The art deco influence is much in evidence with the Egyptian-style motif of the finials and handle form.

AMERICAN STYLES

In North and South America, silver followed the styles established by the colonizing mother country. Canadian silver copied the French fashions, Mexican and South American silver emulated Spanish styles and North American silver generally followed English silver patterns. These European styles were subject to local influences and an unavoidable time lapse between European styles and New World interpretation.

Silver was not discovered in the United States until 1850. Mexico and South America had earlier been discovered to contain large silver deposits, which originally attracted the English to explore North America in the 17th century. However, silver was discovered in Nevada, far from the colonized eastern seaboard. Otherwise, silver coins and other objects were the main source of material for the smiths of the north.

As one would expect of such a vast geographical area as America, colonized by imigrants from a variety of European countries, different cities developed individual styles depending on their own particular influences.

New England and its surrounding colonies became the established centre of the North American silver industry. By the 1860s Boston boasted a large number of London-trained silversmiths, who in turn trained their indigenous successors. The new colonial silver tended to be simpler in style than the

ABOVE

Square waiter, made by Peter David, Philadelphia, *c.* 1730. Square, with cusped corners and a double bead-moulded brim, on shaped and cusped bracket feet, the base engraved with weight.

LEFT

Coffee pot (left) by John McMullin and sugar urn (right) by Christian Wiltberger, both made *c.* 1790 in Philadelphia. These are taken from English patterns of the 1780s and 1790s, drawing on neo-classical styles prevailing in England and then in America. Note the delicate beaded borders. Both are urn-forms with urn-shaped finials, and the coffee pot has a pierced gallery and acanthus-carved wood handle.

English originals, with the emphasis on form and proportion rather than on decoration. Many citizens who had the means to do so, preferred to import silver and other decorative objects from England.

From the 1600s through to the 1850s articles produced were created by silversmiths without many of the new manufacturing methods adopted by their British contemporaries. The results varied greatly in terms of technique and aesthetics. This lack of uniformity makes it hard to put a monetary value upon pieces compared to their English counterparts.

Silver from New York, the second major silverware-producing city, was an intriguing mixture of English, French and Dutch styles. The Dutch influence was due to the colonization of The New Netherlands by settlers from Holland and prevailed long after it became an English colony in 1664 and was rechristened New York. Ideals from France were introduced by Huguenot craftsmen who settled and worked in New York in the late 1700s and also by those fleeing post-Revolutionary France a century later. The French also established themselves in New Orleans, Detroit and Mobile.

As the population spread itself across America, new silver centres were established, notably in Salem, Massachusetts; Lancaster, Pennsylvania; Newport, Rhode Island and Annapolis, Maryland. However, none of the provincial silversmiths made goods of the quality established by the makers of Boston, New York and, in due course, Philadelphia.

Unfortunately, the War of Independence (1773–81) and the 10 years following practically brought the silver industry to a standstill until the economy improved. The next war with Britain in 1812 over Indian and Canadian territorial disputes had a similar effect. Despite the revolution and split from its mother country, America continued to follow English styles.

Philadelphia, another refuge for French emigrés, was by now firmly established as a centre for silver manufacture. The rococo and later the Empire styles were favoured, rather than the more restrained designs of the Boston smiths.

The 19th century saw the establishment of many great firms such as Samuel Kirk and Sons of Baltimore, Gorman Co of Rhode Island and Tiffany & Co of New York. As these companies grew in stature they triumphed over the independent craftsmen of the day.

Although American silver design had progressed, and developed a distinct national character, the most prominent companies imported designers from Europe to head their workshops.

After 1850, mass production resulted in poor silverware. Only a few firms, such as Gorman & Co or Tiffany & Co, managed to produce goods of fine design and good craftsmanship.

BELOW LEFT

Silver tankard, made by Edward Winslow, Boston, *c.* 1705. The low-domed circular cover has a gadrooned moulding, a crenellated lip, and a dolphin-and-mask thumbpiece; the S-scroll handle has a molded and crimped-wire hinge, a rat-tail join, and a winged-cherub terminal. The cast mount, finial and thumbpiece show a Dutch influence.

BELOW

Porringer made by Paul Revere II, Boston, 1760–1790. This was typical of Dutch pieces of the period – circular with a pierced keyhole handle.

RIGHT

Two vases and one centrepiece bowl in green glass with silver overlay decoration, *c.* 1900. The shape of the left-hand vase is interesting as this is the kind of form more usually associated with art nouveau-style cameo glass of the kind made by the studios of Gallé and Daum. It clearly illustrates how the American public were always receptive to new and unusual styles. The vase in the middle successfully combines an almost classical form with sinuous, organic, interlocking floral decoration. The bowl on the right achieves the same effects but reversed onto a horizontal form. This piece would have been used to hold floral centrepiece decorations on the dining-room table.

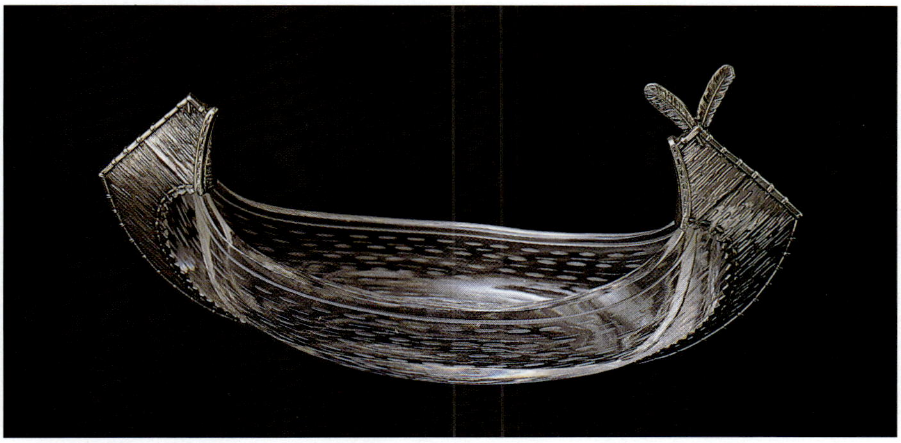

LEFT

Sterling silver and glass butter dish in the form of a canoe, Gorham & Co, *c.* 1895. This canoe-shaped dish typifies the urban American's growing consciousness of the nation's ethnic history. Much of the success of 'Red Indian'-inspired designs lay in the romantic image of the 'Wild West' that was rapidly growing along the Eastern seaboard. To many Americans, Indians survived in place-names only.

LEFT

Six-piece silver tea and coffee service made by Dominick and Haffe, New York, 1880. This highly ornamented hand-chased set with its florid decorations was a most typical and uniquely American design.

QUEEN ANNE TO ROCOCO

Tankards were particularly popular pieces, and following their design development is a good way of monitoring changes of style. In the thriving silver centre of Boston, the clean, pure lines and chastened decoration prevalent between 1690 and 1720, began to be replaced by the pear-shaped, domed lid and finials of the Queen Anne style. In contrast, tankard fashions in New York still favoured a flat lid set with a coin, a traditional scroll handle elaborated by added embossing and a corkscrew thumbpiece. But, between 1720 and 1745, the silverware produced by the New York and Boston silversmiths developed along more similar lines.

The English fashion for tea and coffee pots became popular in America in the first quarter of the 18th century. On the whole, pots made in Boston and Philadelphia tended to have apple- or bullet-shaped bodies while those from New York resembled elongated pears. The functional pear shape proved to have the greater longevity, and evolved into the 'double-bellied' shape of the rococo 'Chippendale' style, in vogue from 1750 to 1790. These rococo pots were also characterized by their low-moulded pedestal foot, finial-topped lid and the C-shaped, scrolled handle made of ebony. The first tea caddies and canisters also appeared during this period.

Lavishly decorated rococo silver tableware and household ornaments adorned the houses of the prosperous and influential merchant class. The confident curves, stylized acanthus leaves, reeding and pineapple finials enlivened the pieces they chose to commission. Pierced scrolls and natural motifs such as shells abounded on centrepieces, monteiths (bowls for cooling wine glasses) and other large objects.

FEDERAL AND EMPIRE SILVER

The neo-classical motifs of the Federal style replaced the exuberance of rococo during the first years of the new American republic in the 1790s. The new style, whose principal embellishments were reeding, fluting and gadrooning, was a complete change of direction. Shape and use of decorations varied between cities. Cream jugs, sugar basins, and tea or coffee pots were first produced as matching services during the Federal period, sometimes with the addition of a tea caddy, tongs, strainer, tea scoop and tray.

The opulent Empire style was fashionable during the 1820s and 30s. Body shapes became round or vase-shaped rather than oval or ovoid, spouts grew more curvacious and often ended as the head of a mythical beast, and lids became elongated, moulded and often highly chased with leaves and other plant forms. Moulding and chasing were more extravagant than ever.

BELOW
Two Empire sauceboats by Anthony Rasch, made in Philadelphia in 1808–19. The serpent handles, the fanned animal spout openings, and the intricate borders are drawn from French designs from the previous 20 years.

VICTORIAN STYLING AND ART SILVER

The transition from the highly decorative Empire mode to the florid exuberance of American Victorian styling was an easy one; the old melted into the new.

New Orleans had emerged as the leadig centre of silver-making in the South. Its silver work was airy and ornate, characterized by beading, latticework and gadrooning, and items such as cake baskets, epergnes and card holders.

Many styles enjoyed a revival during the 1800s:– Greek, Egyptian, rococo, Empire and Renaissance. Heavy Gothic- and Italianate-influenced silver was designed by all the silver centres from the late 1850s into the 70s.

America's two greatest silver companies, Gorham & Co and Tiffany & Co, were founded in 1831 and 1834 respectively. By the 1870s, both were manufacturing in large capacity, shifting away from their European-oriented designs and turning to the Far East for inspiration. Both companies embraced the Japanese decorative arts and popularized cherry blossom, bamboo, fans and bird motifs. These were in demand until the end of the century and were widely imitated. Much of the work was executed in mixed metal combinations such as enamel etched with silver and gold, silver set with gold, copper and brass appliqué, copper with silver chastening, and silver inlaid with semi-precious stones.

Gradually the fluid lines of art nouveau replaced the oriental fashion. Enamel work, swirled decoration and undulating and linked lines featured strongly on caskets, bowls and vases; silver caryatids supported clocks, lamps and irridescent glass bowls; cutlery sets were adorned with naturalistic motifs throughout. It should be said that Tiffany's and Gorman's did not have the entire market to themselves. Other worthy firms and individual silversmiths were busy producing fine pieces of oriental and art nouveau silver.

The art nouveau style was destined to dominate silver design until the second decade of the 20th century, and has a popular following of collectors today.

LEFT

Presentation centrepiece by Tiffany & Co, New York, *c.* 1864. The reeded columnar support is surmounted by a flaring cylindrical stem chased with acanthus leaves supporting a central glass dish. This is flanked by four Greek-key arms with anthemia supporting cylindrical supports for four glass dishes. The base is a reeded urn-form, applied with four rams' heads and a Greek-key border. This centrepiece incorporates both French and English neo-classical Revivalist forms which were used over 50 years before. Designed by John C and Edward C Moore for the Hudson River Railroad Company, it was probably a commission reflecting the owner's personal taste.

AMERICAN STYLE AND ART SILVER

ABOVE

Pair of sterling silver three-branch candelabras, J E Calderwell & Co, *c.* 1880. These pieces display a number of classical influences often found in 19th century European silver, but somehow achieve a more pleasing lightness of form.

BELOW

Silver plate water pitcher, attributed to Reed & Barton, Taunton, Mass, in tusk form, with spot-hammered surface repoussé, chased with foliage in Japanese style and applied with cast dragonflies, *c.* 1885. Shown with: Sterling silver mug in barrel form with a curved handle, spot-hammered with repoussé decoration in Japanese style and chased with pond, water plants and dragonfly, Dominic & Haff, *c.* 1882. These pieces clearly illustrate the unabating thirst for the Japanese style in American tableware. It is also interesting to note that the form of the pitcher is taken from a different medium, that of the inlaid ivory elephant tusks decorated with mother-of-pearl and various other inlays collectively known as *Shibyama*.

RIGHT

Set of 12 coffee spoons in sterling silver and gilt, each individually styled with animal decoration, Shiebler, *c.* 1880. This set of spoons, while having a certain amount of rarity value resting in its completeness and originality, is another very typical example of the lengths American silversmiths went to in their newly adopted oriental 'art' form. As is plainly illustrated here, every single piece in this matching 'set' is in fact totally different, but the harmony of form is continuous throughout. Other than the shapes themselves their main device is to employ variations on a naturalistic theme, ranging from the almost ubiquitous – in Japan – crane, to the bats so beloved by the English Arts & Crafts Movement. It is worth noting that the reverse of every piece is engraved with the single letter 'F', and in keeping with the design principles, the range of lettering itself goes through 12 variations.

BELOW

Sterling silver three-piece tea service decorated with gilt oriental borders, Gorham & Co, 1872. This is an extremely good example of the combination of Japanese inspiration and Western form.

RIGHT

Rare five-piece enamelled tea service by Tiffany & Co, New York 1899–1902. This wonderful expression of naturalist styles also draws on oriental influences in the shape of the etched arabesques and pointed arch panels.

NOTABLE AMERICAN SILVERSMITHS

John Coney (1655–1722), Massachusetts
Gerit Boelen (c. 1645–1729), New York
Bartholomew LeRoux (1663–1713), New York (?)
Simeon Soumaine (1685–1750), New York (?)
Myer Myers (1723–95), New York
Daniel Henchman (1730–75), New York
Paul Revere (1734–1818), Boston
Benjamin Hurt (1729–1815), Boston
Philip Synge, Jr (1703–89), Philadelphia
Philip Hulbeart (1750–64), Philadelphia
Joseph Richardson (1711–84), Philadelphia
Richard Humphreys (1771–96), Philadelphia
Ephraim Brasher (1744–1810), New York
Daniel van Vorhis and Gerrit Schank (fl 1791–93), New York
Simon Bayley (1789–96), New York
William Forbes (1751–1831), Philadelphia
John and James Black, (no dates given), Philadelphia
Adolphe Himmel (fl 1851–65), New Orleans
Christopher Kuchler (fl 1852–9), New Orleans

PROMINENT MANUFACTURING COMPANIES

Gorham & Company: Rhode Island, New York, San Francisco and Chicago
Tiffany & Company, New York
Ball, Black & Co (Black, Starr & Frost until 1876)
The Whiting Manufacturing Company, North Attleboro, Mass.
Wallace Bros, Silver Company, Connecticut
Dominick & Haff, Newark and New Jersey
Hyde & Goodrich, New Orleans
Samuel Kirk & Sons, Baltimore
Wood & Hughes, New York
International Silver Company; Meriden, Connecticut
Reed & Barton; Taunton, Massachusetts

LEFT

Five serving pieces: Left to right: Tiffany & Co sterling silver and gilt berry spoon with cast grape motif handle. Gorham & Co, sterling silver flowerhead spoon. Whiting MFG Co, sterling silver server with cast flowers, and silver ladle with trefoil bowl and bull's head handle. Shiebler sterling silver cakeslice. All *c.* 1885. These display the variety of form in American flatware and the pragmatic approach of making form subservient to purpose. This is best seen in the practical shape of the berry serving spoon and the equally practical and unusual trefoil shape of the consommé ladle.

Care and cleaning hints

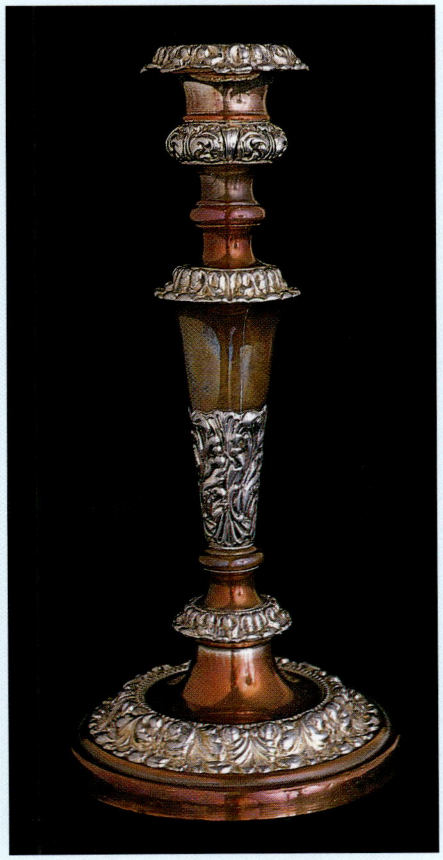

LEFT

Silver candlestick before and after replating. This is a relatively inexpensive process, and can prolong the life of a treasured piece.

TARNISH AND ITS PREVENTION

Tarnish is a natural and inevitable process which occurs to sterling silver, Old Sheffield Plate and electroplate. The time silver takes to tarnish depends entirely on the amount of humidity and pollutants present in the atmosphere.

Regular cleaning and polishing will restore the shine to silver and will help prevent tarnishing. Similarly, measures can be taken to preserve the lustre of objects not on permanent display or in regular use. These can be kept in tarnish-proof bags available from jewellers and department stores. Another solution is to wrap articles in acid-free tissue paper and place them in plastic bags, making them as airtight as possible before storage. Tarnish-preventative material, available from fabric shops, can also be used to line cupboards.

Do not be tempted to wrap silver in cling film (plastic wrap); certain brands cause a chemical reaction which can permanently discolour your silver.

CLEANING TECHNIQUES – PAST AND PRESENT

Fortunately, cleaning silver today is no longer the drudgery it once was in the past. It was the responsibility of the butler or other household servants to clean silver plate using a variety of favoured preparations such as pumice, chalk and ammonia. It was also common practice to clean silver using the thumb or palm of the hand to remove tarnish and create lustre. This basic, but somewhat tiring, technique was known as 'butler's hand'.

That doyenne of household management, Mrs Beeton, advised Victorian housemaids first to remove grease from household silver with a strong lather of common yellow soap and boiling water. This was followed by the application of a thick paste of hartshorn powder mixed with cold water and spirits of wine which was left to dry, brushed off with a soft plate-brush and then buffered with a dry leather. She was strongly against the use of cleaning preparations containing quicksilver (mercury) 'as it made plate extremely brittle'.

The change in social conditions in this century led polish manufacturers – with varying degrees of success – to develop cleaning preparations to cut down the amount of time and elbow grease needed to clean silver. Foam polishes without any abrasive content can produce very effective and pleasing results with little effort. These are normally applied with a sponge and then rinsed off, removing tarnish and leaving a good finish without the polish build-up that occurs with some cleaning products. Various polishes contain non-toxic tarnish inhibitors that keep silver clean for up to three times longer than polish without inhibitors.

A nail or toothbrush can be used to apply polish or foam to highly-detailed or pierced articles. When rinsing, the brush can be used to clean out the same intricate areas. Thoroughly dry the article immediately to avoid streaking.

For those with an expanding collection, silver dip can be purchased in gallon containers and, although principally manufactured for hotel use, it can be ordered from many hardware stores. Silver dips are powerful but, if used properly, they will not harm your silver. Keep the dip in a lidded plastic bucket, preferably in a garage or outside shed since the smell is rather pungent. Never store the liquid in a metal bucket.

Pieces for cleaning should be agitated in the dip for a few seconds, removed, and then rinsed in cold water immediately. Use only cold water since hot or warm water will cause the silver to yellow, requiring cleaning with a conventional polish to remove the yellow effect. The dip should eliminate tarnish from even the most inaccessable parts but, should stubborn tarnish still linger in crevices, use either a natural bristle brush or a cloth soaked in the dip to shift it. After rinsing, use foam polish for a quick once-over as it contains tarnish inhibitors not incorporated in the dip. Finally, rinse and dry.

A note of caution. Some American dips are known to leave an unwelcome bloom on silver. But this can be removed by using a regular cream polish.

Good reports have been received of a new cleaning method recently launched. It involves placing a metal sheet in water with soda crystals. This mixture instantly removes tarnish on contact. Another product widely available in the USA and UK actually puts silver back onto articles. It is especially useful for 'touching-up' plated goods that are beginning to expose their base metal. However, cautious use is needed to maintain the silver surface. Since the use of any other polish will remove the silver build-up, this is hardly a cost-effective way of replating an article.

Difficult tea and coffee stains are best tackled by soaking overnight in a solution of warm water, and soda crystals according to the manufacturer's instructions. The crystals can be purchased from any chemist or hardware store. Glass claret jugs, crystal decanters and cruet bottles are best soaked in warm water and denture cleaning tablets – an old trick of the trade. These tablets are extremely effective not only at cleaning the glass or crystal but also any stains from silver attachments.

Lacquer As Protection

During the Victorian era, lacquer – then a mixture of varnish of shellac dissolved in alcohol – was used as a protective coating for large and highly decorative pieces of silver which were constantly on display. The clear lacquer sealed the object from the air and therefore completely retarded the tarnishing process. Today a similar coating is usually composed of cellulose or silicone. The old-fashioned lacquer had a tendency to turn yellow with age, resulting in dulled and greyed silver – thereby defeating the object of the exercise. Modern lacquers are not prone to such discolouration.

The most effectivce method of lacquering is by baking it on. This is not suitable, however, for pieces that have any soft solder points or a soft base metal, as baking will cause these to melt. The parts may drop off or the whole piece break down altogether! The alternative is spraying – but interior spraying can leave tiny pinholes in the lacquer, which allows air in beneath the coating. The resultant tarnishing cannot be removed by hand cleaning, and necessitates professional removal of the lacquer. Lacquering is generally not recommended for articles that have a culinary purpose, since all lacquers are toxic and erode with use.

Despite these cautions, good lacquering provides a highly satisfactory finish for suitable objects, but professional advice is essential before committing an object for treatment. To clean a lacquered piece, simply wipe with a damp cloth – and it's gleaming. That's the plus point for good lacquering!

REPLATING

Replating can be a relatively inexpensive process. The depth of plating is measured in microns and – for hollow-ware items, such as meat platters which are used for carving – it is recommended that you ask for a 20- to 30-micron silver coating. Items such as coffee pots and salvers are unlikely to receive such extreme use and will require somewhere between 10 and 15 microns, depending on whether you wish the plating to last about 15 to 20 years.

Just how long plating lasts depends on how it is cleaned. Products with a high abrasive content will obviously erode silver faster than more gentle solutions.

PITTING

Items that come into contact with salt or fruit acid are prone to pitting (black spots). To prevent this, wash and dry pieces straight after use. Do not leave them to soak.

If pitting has occurred and it cannot be removed by silver polish alone, take the object to a reputable silversmith for restoration. Good silversmiths can be found by the recommendations of the silver trade journals or by silver experts. Quotations should always be asked for before work begins. The expert will probably recommend that silver objects have the spots polished out. Plated objects can also be polished but there is a danger of going through to the base metal, which will then necessitate replating. If the object is Old Sheffield Plate, the restoration should be considered carefully; polishing may take away too much silver and replating will be detrimental to its value and appearance. It is best to leave Old Sheffield Plate as it is, unless advised otherwise.

If you do need to restore old silver, ask for an 'antique finish', in keeping with the age of the piece.

The insides of salt cellars and fruit dishes can be gold-plated, as gold is impervious to pitting and looks decorative. Gold-plating is not permanent and can be removed professionally. It is not recommended that Old Sheffield Plate items are treated in this way as the modern method of gold-plating was never used in the original production process. Gold-plate is subject to slight discoloration which can be removed with a damp cloth; any lingering marks can be removed with non-abrasive foam silver polish.

LEFT
The effect of salt corrosion on silver. When this occurs, it may be necessary to have the piece restored by a professional.

BELOW LEFT
The results of machine-polishing on the same article. This method is not recommended on plated objects, particulaly Old Sheffield Plate, as there is a danger that the silver will be worn away and reveal the base metal underneath.

BELOW
A badly scratched tray. If the piece is sterling silver, scratches can be removed by machine-polishing. Plated objects may require replating, while Old Sheffield Plate is best left alone.

SCRATCHES

Trays, salvers and platters are especially prone to scratching. Badly scratched sterling silver items can be taken to a silversmith where the marks can be removed. Electroplated articles are more difficult to deal with in this respect, as machine-polishing may remove the silver surface. Re-plating is normally required for these pieces. An expert can advise. Leave Old Sheffield Plate as it is.

DISHWASHERS AND SILVER

Sterling silver flatware can be put in the dishwasher following the machine manufacturers' recommendations. Keep them separate from stainless steel items as a reaction can occur, tarnishing the silver and corroding the stainless steel. If salt is used as a water softener in the machine then do not place any silverware in it. The salt is extremely corrosive.

Some items such as knives have handles filled with pitch or tar. If heated in a dishwasher the filling could expand and split the handle. Modern equivalents are filled with substances suitable for machine use. Always check manufacturers' instructions before trying items in the dishwasher.

Similarly, servers with mother-of-pearl or ivory or bone handles should never be put in the dishwasher.

HAND WASHING

Silver and plate used to serve food is best washed in warm soapy water, rinsed and dried after use. Abrasive scourers and cleaning products must be avoided, as they will scratch the surface of your silver and spoil its appearance.

Index

SELECTED BIBLIOGRAPHY

Antique Collector, "The Complex Story of the Search for a Modern Style in Silver 1880–1919"; Nicholas Roots, October 1981
The Antique Dealer & Collectors' Guide, "From Modernism to the Contemporary", Jaqueline Pruskin, August 1983
Culme, John; *Nineteenth-Century Silver*, Country Life Books, 1977
Grimwade, Arthur; *Rococo Silver 1727–1765*, Faber & Faber, 1974
Krekel-Aalberse, Annelies; *Art Nouveau and Art Deco Silver*, Thames and Hudson, 1989
Hayward, J F; *Huguenot Silver in England 1688–1727*, Faber & Faber 1959
Hughes, Eleanor; *Silver for Collectors*, Treasure Press, 1990
Hughes, Graham; *Modern Silver throughout the World 1880–1967*, Studio Vista, 1967
Luddington, John; *Starting to Collect Silver*, Antique Collectors' Club, 1988
Oman, Charles; *English Domestic Silver*, A & C Black, 1967
Rainwater, Dorothy T, *Encyclopedia of American Silver Manufacturers'*, Crown Publishers, 1975
Rowe, Robert; *Adam Silver (1765–1795)*, Faber & Faber, 1965
Sutton, Arthur; *A Edward Jones*, A Edward Jones ltd, 1980
Wenham, Edward; *Old Silver for Modern Settings*, G Bell & Sons ltd, 1950
Wyler, Seymour B; *The Book of Old Sheffield Plate*, Crown Publishers
Wyler, Seymour B; *Old Silver*, Crown Publishers, 1965

ACKNOWLEDGEMENTS

The author and publishers would like to thank the following:

Julia Laflin for her constant assistance and research; Nicholas Harris of the Silver and Decorative Arts Gallery, King's Road, London, for providing information on 19th- and 20th-century American silver, and for permitting his extensive collection to be photographed; Peter Waldron of Sotheby's; Adam Langford for advice on fakes and hallmarks; Fiona Rhodes; Eric Delieb; Grace Seymour-Cole of Adam's Room Antiques, Wimbledon; J A Campbell Silversmiths, London; CJ Vander & Co, London; William Comyns of London; OG Plating; Ronald Schindler and Laurence Langford for providing me with the opportunity to write this book.

PICTURE CREDITS

Although the majority of photographs were taken at Langford's, the author and publishers would like to thank Sotheby's and Christies, and the following silver dealers from the London Silver Vaults, Chancery House, Chancery Lane, for providing access to their collections for photography:

S Baulker of Shure's; L Block; P Bloom; L Brian; E Bryan of Franks; B Collins; P Daniels; D Golding; J Hamilton; B Lampert; J Lesley of Percy's; I Leon of Leon Antiques; L Miller of H Miller Antiques ltd; the Linden clan; C and T Mammon; J Mammon; J Simon; L Smith of Rare Arts and E & CT Koufman; H Stern of Silstar; S and J Stodel; R Walters.

Hallmarks reproduced by kind permission of Crown Publishers, New York

Black and white photographs courtesy of Northend Publications, Sheffield.

Jacket photograph: Angelo Hornak/Private Collection.